BOOK 2

Her Name Is Woman

GIEN KARSSEN

NAVPRESS

A MINISTRY OF THE NAVIGATORS

P.O. Box 6000, Colorado Springs, Colorado 80934

The Navigators is an international, evangelical Christian organization. Jesus Christ gave His followers the Great Commission to go and make disciples (Matthew 28:19). The aim of The Navigators is to help fulfill that commission by multiplying laborers for Christ in every nation.

NavPress is the publishing ministry of The Navigators. NavPress publications are tools to help Christians grow. Although publications alone cannot make disciples or change lives, they can help believers learn biblical discipleship, and apply what they learn to their lives and ministries.

English translation © 1977 by The Navigators
All rights reserved
ISBN: 0-89109-424-5

Library of Congress Catalog No. 77-081187

Fifth Printing, 1981

(Originally published in the Netherlands as *Nogmaals Manninne—Vrouwen in de Bijbel,* © Buijten & Schipperheijn, Amsterdam, 1976. ISBN: 90-6064-097-7)

Unless otherwise indicated, Scripture quotations are from the *New American Standard Bible,* © the Lockman Foundation, 1960, 1962, 1963, 1968, 1971, 1972, 1973, and 1975. Other versions used are the *Amplified New Testament,* © the Lockman Foundation 1954, 1958; *The New Testament in Modern English, Revised Edition* by J.B. Phillips, 1958, 1960, 1972; and *The Living Bible,* © 1971 by Tyndale House Publishers, Wheaton, Illinois.

Printed in the United States of America

Contents

Old Testament

New Testament

Dedication

In grateful remembrance
of
my parents

*"If there is anything in my thoughts
or style to commend, the credit is due to
my parents for instilling in me an early love
of the Scriptures."**
DANIEL WEBSTER
(American statesman, 1782-1852)

*From *Halley's Bible Handbook* by Henry H. Halley, page 18. Copyright © 1965
by Halley's Bible Handbook, Inc. Reprinted by permission.

Foreword

All my life I have read about the women of the Bible, learning much from them even though they were somewhat vague, historic characters.

While reading *Her Name Is Woman, Book 2,* these same characters have suddenly come alive. Because of Gien's careful research, sanctified imagination, and skill as a writer, I found myself understanding these women and their situations in a new way.

Knowing more about the customs of their day helps us understand better why they acted as they did.

It is interesting to note that God's women, down through the centuries, have enjoyed a freedom the world will find difficult to understand—the freedom to be and to do that which God intended.

You will find this book both interesting and enlightening.

Ruth Bell Graham
Montreat, North Carolina

Preface

My first book, *Her Name Is Woman,* was limited by its size and therefore could only include a few of the many women in the Bible. Questions like, "What about Ruth or Deborah?" and, "Why wasn't Mary Magdalene mentioned?" were bound to come up. *Her Name Is Woman, Book 2* explores the lives of 25 more biblical women who were not dealt with in the first book.

The Bible should be the guide for every woman searching for the meaning of her existence. In the Scriptures a woman can read that God created her in His own image, and that she can become personally acquainted with Jesus Christ, the Saviour of the world. She will also learn that to function well she must live in close relationship with her Maker. These exciting facts clearly express her deep-down desires and ideals.

Scripture offers guidelines to every woman who longs for a meaningful life, who seeks to become whole and fulfilled. These inborn, inner urges originate from the commission God gave woman at her creation. He expects woman, an equal partner with man, to be willing to take her part in the well-being of the home and society. This book, like the first, illustrates that the spiritual side of a woman is extremely important.

In *Her Name Is Woman, Book 2,* you will discover how

selected women of the Bible fulfilled their tasks and how they carried out their calling. In biblical times, as well as in our own twentieth century, some women succeeded and others failed. The questions we need to ask are "Why?" and "How?"

"These things happened to them as an example, and they were written for our instruction," Paul wrote (1 Corinthians 10:11). So we ought to consider these biblical women as vivid instructions for our lives. We should learn from them, be encouraged, comforted, and warned by them, and meet Jesus Christ through some of their lives.

The reception *Her Name Is Woman* received was encouraging to me. I hope that this book will receive the same warm-hearted acceptance.

You may approach this book in two ways. First, just read it. But be sure to include the Bible passages at the beginning of each chapter in your reading. They are an important part of the book. Second, discuss the book in a small group. Consider the subjects and questions with some other people, in the home or with a small group. This will give added insight into your study of these women.

References at the bottom of many pages will help you dig deeper into the Bible's wealth of truth and wisdom. You may answer the questions at the end of each chapter personally or discuss them with your group. You may also conduct topical studies of these women or research accompanying themes. Whatever your direction might be, you will be stimulated as you discuss these women with others, especially after your own individual preparation.

I trust that meeting these women will turn out to be a happy surprise for you, and that you will notice how up-to-date and relevant their experiences are to yours.

I pray that they will show you the way to a richer and happier life with God and other people.

Suggestions

I feel, as many do, that the most fruitful discussion results when small groups of people share what the Bible has said to them personally.

The following suggestions will be helpful for those interested in being in or in leading a Bible study group.

SUGGESTIONS FOR BIBLE STUDY GROUPS

1. Start with a small group—usually with a minimum of six and a maximum of ten people. This way your group will be large enough for an interesting discussion, but small enough for each member to participate. As your number increases, start a second group.

2. Before you start the group, you should decide how often you want to meet. Many people may hesitate to give themselves to something new for an indefinite period of time. This problem can be settled if you decide beforehand to meet, for example, four to six times. If after that time period you decide to continue on, then agree on a number of meetings.

3. Remember that a Bible study group should discuss the Bible. To prevent some from riding hobby horses, it is advisable that each participant prepare her study at home

beforehand. Then the meeting can be used for discussing each person's prepared study. Groups flourish where each member shares her personal findings.

4. Stress the need of applying the lessons learned and help one another in doing this. There is a far greater need for spiritual growth than for an increase of knowledge *per se.* "How can what I learned influence my life?" is a question each participant should ask herself and answer during each discussion.

5. Determine, before you start, to attend every meeting. Miss only when you absolutely cannot attend. If you can't attend, do the study anyhow and make up for it at the next meeting.

6. Consider yourself a member of the group. Feel free to make a contribution. Lack of experience should not keep you from taking part in the discussion. On the other hand, resist the temptation to dominate the group.

SUGGESTIONS FOR LEADERS OF BIBLE STUDY GROUPS

1. Be sure you have given sufficient time to your own Bible study and that you have completed it.

2. Come prepared. Make notes of the points you want to stress. Approach these points with questions.

3. Teach by asking questions instead of by making statements. Few mountain climbers enjoy being carried to the top. Leave the joy of climbing to them. Don't do all the talking. Guide the discussion in such a way that each member of the group can participate.

4. Prepare thought-provoking questions. Ask questions which apply the Bible to daily life problems. Omit questions which can be answered by a simple yes or no.

5. Arrange your time and seating arrangement beforehand. (A circle is generally the best.) Begin and end on time. Unobtrusively keep your eye on your watch.

6. Pray for yourself and for each member of the group.

Pray that Christ will speak to each person present by His Word. Pray that the Holy Spirit will make you sensitive to the needs of others. Prayer results in enthusiasm, and this is absolutely essential for the success of your discussion.

These suggestions are not limited to a certain type of Bible study group. You can use the same principles for the study of Bible books, chapters, or biblical subjects.*

SUGGESTIONS FOR A GROUP DISCUSSION ABOUT HAGAR (an example for all the chapters)

1. Be sure that every member of the group has completed her own study. Encourage each to take notes during the discussion.

2. Decide ahead of time that you as a group will restrict yourselves to answering only the given Bible study questions or closely related subjects.

3. Let every discussion center around the Bible. Always ask, "What does the Bible say about this subject?"

4. The success of each Bible group discussion is strongly dependent on the questions the leader asks and on how she starts and guides the conversation. Four types of questions are:

    a. Questions to start the discussion.

    b. Questions to guide the discussion.

    c. Questions that help clarify and deepen the subject.

    d. Questions which stimulate application.

5. Examples of the above questions as pertaining to Hagar:

    a. Questions to start the discussion:

       (1) What did we learn about Hagar?

*For practical guidelines on this, see *The Navigator Bible Studies Handbook* (NavPress, 1979). This book explains several simple methods for analytical Bible study, along with important principles.

(2) What were the consequences of Sarah's willfulness?

(3) What did we learn about obedience?

(4) How can we apply Christ's love to our own needs?

When you introduce every main point of the study this way, you will avoid getting the stated Bible study questions parroted back and you will guarantee an interesting discussion. It is wise to summarize one point before going on to the next.

b. Questions to guide the discussion:

(1) What did someone else discover?

(2) Does anyone else have anything to add?

(3) Is there anyone else who wishes to say something?

Address the whole group with these sorts of questions, not just one person in particular. This provides an open discussion in which everyone present can participate.

c. Questions that help clarify and deepen the subject:

(1) What does obedience to God entail?

(2) What do you think was Hagar's main fault?

Prepare these questions in view of the emphasis the group needs most. Have Bible verses ready to help find the right answers. Ask these questions at the proper place in the discussion under the questions mentioned above in 5a (in this instance in 5a3).

d. Questions which stimulate application:

(1) What do you consider the most important warning in this story?

(2) How does this affect your life personally?

Since questions on application can be asked last in the Bible discussion, you can, going around the circle, expect each member of the group to give her personal answer. Words to keep in mind while asking questions are: what, how, why, when.

6. Make a time schedule for yourself to guarantee that

every part of the discussion receives sufficient attention. Reserve enough time for those points you think are of utmost importance. Since the last question of the Bible study is an application question, you may want to emphasize it.

7. Shy participants often can be drawn into the discussion by asking them to read a Bible verse. It is difficult to control those who want to dominate the discussion. Calling for contributions from others often helps. "What do others think?" would be an example of this type of approach. Sometimes it is necessary to talk privately with the over talkative person, explaining the necessity of group participation. Getting back on track when the subject begins to wander can be done by saying, "Perhaps we could discuss this further after the study," or, "Let us, as we agreed, try to stick to our subject of the study."

8. Sharing the application is the most important part of your discussion. Be sure to allow sufficient time for each person present to answer the last stated question. The answer to that question should be personal, specific, and practical. An example of an application in connection with Hagar could be, "The most important principle for me to consider is that Jesus Christ loves me and cares about my needs. Therefore I need to trust Him continually and let Him know my problems and my joys."

9. If you close the discussion with a time of prayer, pray about the things you have discussed. For example, pray for your own application or for someone else's. Don't force anything. Encourage short prayers. Someone who is too shy to pray aloud could enter in by saying, "Amen." As the openness of the group increases, so will the prayer. Then other points can be added for intercession.

10. Close with the promise that at the beginning of the next meeting time will be given for sharing experiences in connection with your group's applications.

These guidelines can be used for all the group discussions about the women in this book.

Biography

Gien Karssen was raised in a Christian home and became a Christian at the age of 12 as a result of her parents' lives and training. After she had been married only six weeks, the Germans interned her husband in a concentration camp where he died. Just before his death he inscribed Luke 9:62 in his diary, "But Jesus said to him, 'No one, after putting his hand to the plow and looking back, is fit for the kingdom of God.' " This verse challenged Gien and has given purpose and direction to her life.

She met Dawson Trotman, founder of The Navigators, in 1948 in Doorn, Holland. She started the Navigator ministry there by translating The Navigators *Topical Memory System* into Dutch and handling all the enrollments. Over the years she has worked in many capacities with The Navigators. Girls who have been personally helped by Gien can be found on almost every continent of the globe.

Gien is a popular speaker, Bible study leader, trainer of women, and has many years of experience as a free-lance writer for Christian periodicals in Europe. *Her Name Is Woman, Book 2* is her second book and is a sequel to her bestselling *Her Name Is Woman, Book 1* in her studies on the women of the Bible. The first book has been translated into several languages and is currently being used as a Bible study aid around the world.

Old Testament

1

Hagar,
whose extreme need was met
by Jesus Christ

Genesis 16:1-16 Now Sarai, Abram's wife had borne him no children, and she had an Egyptian maid whose name was Hagar. So Sarai said to Abram, "Now behold, the Lord has prevented me from bearing children. Please go in to my maid; perhaps I shall obtain children through her." And Abram listened to the voice of Sarai.

And after Abram had lived ten years in the land of Canaan, Abram's wife Sarai took Hagar the Egyptian, her maid, and gave her to her husband Abram as his wife. And he went in to Hagar, and she conceived; and when she saw that she had conceived, her mistress was despised in her sight. And Sarai said to Abram, "May the wrong done me be upon you. I gave my maid into your arms; but when she saw that she had conceived, I was despised in her sight. May the Lord judge between you and me." But Abram said to Sarai, "Behold, your maid is in your power; do to her what is good in your sight." So Sarai treated her harshly, and she fled from her presence.

Now the angel of the Lord found her by a spring of water in the wilderness, by the spring on the way to Shur. And he

*From *The Women of the Bible* by Herbert Lockyer, page 62. Copyright © 1967 by Zondervan Publishing House. Used by permission

said, "Hagar, Sarai's maid, where have you come from and where are you going?" And she said, "I am fleeing from the presence of my mistress Sarai." Then the angel of the Lord said to her, "Return to your mistress, and submit yourself to her authority." Moreover, the angel of the Lord said to her, "I will greatly multiply your descendants so that they shall be too many to count." The angel of the Lord said to her further, "Behold, you are with child, and you shall bear a son; and you shall call his name Ishmael, because the Lord has given heed to your affliction. And he will be a wild donkey of a man, his hand will be against everyone, and everyone's hand will be against him; and he will live to the east of all his brothers."

Then she called the name of the Lord who spoke to her, "Thou art a God who sees"; for she said, "Have I even remained alive here after seeing Him?" Therefore the well was called Beer-lahai-roi; behold, it is between Kadesh and Bered. So Hagar bore Abram a son; and Abram called the name of his son, whom Hagar bore, Ishmael. And Abram was eighty-six years old when Hagar bore Ishmael to him.

Genesis 21:1-21 Then the Lord took note of Sarah as He had said, and the Lord did for Sarah as He had promised. So Sarah conceived and bore a son to Abraham in his old age, at the appointed time of which God had spoken to him. And Abraham called the name of his son who was born to him, whom Sarah bore to him, Isaac. Then Abraham circumcised his son Isaac when he was eight days old, as God had commanded him. Now Abraham was one hundred years old when his son Isaac was born to him.

And Sarah said, "God has made laughter for me; everyone who hears will laugh with me." And she said, "Who would have said to Abraham that Sarah would nurse children? Yet I have borne him a son in his old age." And the child grew and was weaned, and Abraham made a great feast on the day that Isaac was weaned.

Now Sarah saw the son of Hagar the Egyptian, whom she had borne to Abraham, mocking. Therefore she said to Abraham, "Drive out this maid and her son, for the son of this maid shall not be an heir with my son Isaac." And the matter distressed Abraham greatly because of his son. But God said to Abraham, "Do not be distressed because of the lad and your maid; whatever Sarah tells you, listen to her, for through Isaac your descendants shall be named. And of the son of the maid I will make a nation also, because he is your descendant."

So Abraham rose early in the morning, and took bread and a skin of water, and gave them to Hagar, putting them on her shoulder, and gave her the boy, and sent her away. And she departed, and wandered about in the wilderness of Beersheba. And the water in the skin was used up, and she left the boy under one of the bushes. Then she went and sat down opposite him, about a bowshot away, for she said, "Do not let me see the boy die." And she sat opposite him, and lifted up her voice and wept. And God heard the lad crying; and the angel of God called to Hagar from heaven, and said to her, "What is the matter with you, Hagar? Do not fear, for God has heard the voice of the lad where he is. Arise, lift up the lad, and hold him by the hand; for I will make a great nation of him." Then God opened her eyes and she saw a well of water; and she went and filled the skin with water, and gave the lad a drink. And God was with the lad, and he grew; and he lived in the wilderness, and became an archer. And he lived in the wilderness of Paran; and his mother took a wife for him from the land of Egypt.

Hagar plodded slowly along the rough path. Her chafed feet and ankles hurt with each step and the seams of her long robe were frayed and torn. Her heart beat quickly from the exertion of her long journey; her eyes burned from the scorching glare of the sun.

The wilderness in which she walked day after day offered no protection. During the day terrible heat rose off the sand in vapors and the fierce wind blew dust into her mouth and nose. At night the temperature dropped and the land became bitterly cold.

In spite of the risks, Hagar pressed on toward Egypt, her home country. She wanted to return to the place where Sarah, the wife of Abraham (as they were later named), had bought her about 25 years before and then taken her to Canaan as a slave.

While she walked, she reflected on the years which had passed. They had been good years. Even though a slave girl, she had enjoyed a good life. *After all,* she thought, *I have been privileged to live with Abraham and Sarah, with whom God has even made a special covenant.* Through their example, she had come in contact with the living God.

Despite the good memories of her past, no thoughts of gratitude stirred Hagar's mind now. Far from that! Feeling that she had been wronged and even insulted, she was in a bitter frame of mind.

In a strange way, Hagar was suffering the consequences of a bad situation in Abraham's household. When he had moved from the land between the Euphrates and the Tigris Rivers to Canaan, God had promised him a son. Through that son, Abraham was told that he would become the father of a multitude of nations.[1]

But years passed and the son didn't come. Worried, Sarah got the idea that the promised child should be born to a concubine, a second wife, instead of to her. According to the laws of that time, such a practice was allowed. In fact, a baby born of this arrangement was legally considered to be the child of the true wife and as such a rightful heir. In order to carry out such a plan, Sarah considered Hagar, who occupied a favorable position within the family circle. After Hagar became Abraham's second wife, it was not long before she told him the happy news, "I am pregnant!"

Before Hagar's pregnancy, Abraham, since he had no son,[2] had thought that the male head of his household, Eliezer, would be his legal heir. But now, through Hagar, the child God had promised him might once again be coming into sight. Though Abraham had reason to expect that his heir would be a son of Sarah, up to that point God had never mentioned to him who the mother would be. He waited 13 years for God to give him the answer.[3]

Before long, it was evident that Sarah's solution had been a purely human one. God's blessing toward Hagar had never been asked for and was not given. Impatient and doubting God's ability to work her situation out, Sarah had

1. Genesis 12:1-5
2. Genesis 15:2-5
3. Genesis 17:15-16

chosen her own way and Abraham had given in too readily to her plans. No wonder the peace of God had left the house.

At this time in history, a childless woman was despised by all. Unfortunately, Hagar didn't miss an opportunity to communicate such feelings toward Sarah. Then, as now, few things in the world were so subtle and yet transmitted so clearly as the feelings of one woman toward another.

Sarah in turn reacted to Hagar's nonverbal communication. She too knew her weapons and how to use them. As the mistress, she had the oldest and first rights, a fact confirmed by the laws of her time. Even now Hagar remained her personal possession, to do with as she pleased.

Unable to approach Hagar without Sarah's permission, Abraham likewise could not prevent Sarah from using her power to humiliate Hagar.

Although all three of them had trespassed God's laws and were equally guilty in His sight, it is understandable that Hagar's attitude hurt Sarah deeply. This hurt partially explains Sarah's terrible treatment of Hagar. Yet, knowledge of Sarah's inner turmoil does not make Hagar's humiliation any easier for us to accept.

Hagar, tiring of Sarah's treatment, finally lost her patience. Without asking permission, she fled to the wilderness. In this way she was true to her name. Hagar literally meant "flight."

Knowing full well that she and her yet unborn child might be heading toward death, she stalked out of the camp. Alone, without food, she knew that she might never reach her homeland. Her child might never see life. But she had to try.

Instinctively she began walking south on the long road toward Egypt. The farther she walked, the more her danger dawned on her. She had given up a sheltered community for the endless, inhospitable wilderness. Neither man nor beast could be seen for miles; there was no one to help her.

Somewhere in the northeastern section of the Sinai Peninsula, Hagar reached a desert spring along the road to

Shur. The oasis offered refreshment and rest, but it did not still her inner needs.

Alone, separated from security and friendship, she cried out from her innermost being to the God of Abraham, the only One who could save her. And He had not abandoned her. The slowly moving dot in the rough desert terrain of the Sinai had not escaped His attention. He had kept His eye on Hagar just like He continues to do for all mankind.

"Hagar," He called loudly, addressing her by her first name.[4] He knew precisely who she was.

"Maid of Sarai," He added, placing her into the framework through which He saw her. In His eyes, she was still Sarah's maid. He did not begin the conversation with a rebuke, though under the circumstances He could have.

"Where have you come from, and where are you going?" He then asked. It was a disarming approach that gave Hagar room to speak her mind freely. Jesus Christ, who during His years on earth would use the same approach with guilty women and win their hearts, was speaking to her.[5] Jesus Christ Himself was visiting her in the person of the Angel of the Lord. It was one of the pre-incarnate appearances of the Lord Jesus in the Old Testament.

Later, He would reveal Himself in the same manner to Abraham, the father of all believers,[6] and to Moses, the Law-giver,[7] both of whom the Bible calls friends of God.[8] Both the Patriarch Jacob and Gideon, the hero of faith, would also be deeply impressed when they met Christ under similar circumstances.[9]

But Jesus Christ's first documented meeting with a person was with Hagar, long before He came to earth to redeem mankind. A young heathen woman who did not belong to the people of God, she—the mother of an unborn child—had come before God in extreme need. God in turn showed her the way to deliverance. In humility and repentance, she obeyed Him and turned back toward Abraham's camp. Her sin, like that of Eve, was pride. Renouncing her proud spirit of rebellion and willful independence, Hagar returned to Sarah her mistress.

---

4. Genesis 16:7-9

5. John 4:4-42; 8:3-11

6. Genesis 17:4-5

7. Exodus 3:2-6

8. James 2:23; Exodus 33:11

9. Genesis 28:12-17; Judges 6:11-23

Instead of asserting herself or speaking out for her own rights, Hagar had to abase herself. The Lord Himself had given her an example of humility when He had stooped down to speak with her. Later, He would humble Himself much more in order to provide sinful people with an alternative to death.[10] He would give new life to everyone who personally trusted in Him to the honor of God.

God, who gives special blessings to those who have the courage to humble themselves,[11] honored Hagar's obedience. "The baby you are expecting is a son," He said. "You are to name him Ishmael [that name meant 'God hears']. You will get a large offspring, Hagar, so large that it cannot be counted."[12]

The son she expected would not be an easy man with whom to get along. He would have a wild and untamed character. Yet how she must have rejoiced in her heart at these words of God. There was hope again. Instead of expecting death, she now had the perspective of life. The future was blossoming for her and her unborn child. Jesus had a plan for their lives and had come down to share it with her personally.

"O God who sees me!" she exclaimed in adoration and worship. Yet she was also afraid and overawed. *I have seen God and am still alive,* she thought after God left her. *I am able to tell others.*

Later, the spring oasis where she encountered God was named Beer-lahai-roi,[13] which translated meant, "the well of the Living One who sees me." Hagar had experienced the true God who saw and answered her during her time of need.

As long as she lived, she no doubt remembered this experience with God. Every time she pronounced Ishmael's name, she reminded herself of the fact: the living God had heard and had acted.

Approximately 17 years passed. Ishmael had now become a strong young man. Isaac, the son of promise, had now been born and at three years of age was finally ready to be weaned.

---

10. Philippians 2:5-11   12. Genesis 16:10-12
11. 1 Peter 5:6   13. Genesis 16:14

The weaning of a child during this time was cause for much celebration, for it was considered to be a milestone in the youngster's life. Abraham's entire household and many of his friends from neighboring cities came to celebrate and to see for themselves the miracle God had performed for Abraham and Sarah. One hundred-year-old Abraham and 90-year-old Sarah had been blessed with a son in their old age, the son of promise from whose offspring the Messiah would later come.

But the party atmosphere was not entirely pleasant. Ishmael, the oldest son, could not tolerate all the attention his younger brother was receiving and began to mock him. There was, of course, more going on behind the scenes than just an innocent rivalry between two brothers. Ishmael, the son of natural birth who was procreated in unbelief and impatience, felt inferior to Isaac, the son of promise. Unwilling to accept second-place billing, Ishmael refused to acknowledge Isaac's privileged position. Unaware of God's promises to his mother in the wilderness many years before, Ishmael could not accept his subservient position.

Abraham loved both boys equally as only a father could. Only Sarah understood what was at stake. "Send the slave girl and her son away," she demanded of Abraham. "I won't have him sharing your inheritance with my son."[14]

In response to his wife's strong statement, Abraham became upset and confused. As he prayed, God showed him that the separation of his sons was necessary. The patriarchal line of the tribe God had chosen for His future people, Israel, would run through Isaac. He alone was the son of God's promise[15] and would become the forefather of a family of 12 tribes. From now on, Abraham came to understand, the difference between both sons had to be clear. Sarah was right. But through this confusion, God's promise to Hagar that her posterity would become great remained valid. Like Isaac, Ishmael would become the father of a family of 12 tribes because he was a son of Abraham.[16]

Thus Abraham had to send Hagar and her son away into the wilderness. After living in Abraham's household for

14. Genesis 21:10
15. Galatians 4:22-23
16. Genesis 25:12-16

nearly 30 years, she was now forced to leave. As Abraham filled up a water skin for Hagar, all three of them realized that the food and water for Hagar and Ishmael would not last long. Nevertheless, the difficult journey began.

The inevitable came all too quickly. The water supply ran out and, despite their frenzied searches, Hagar and Ishmael could not find a spring. Ishmael, weakened from walking and dehydration, was the first to fall to the ground, exhausted. When it became clear that her son would soon die, Hagar used the last of her strength to drag him beneath a small but sheltering bush. It was the final service she could render to her child.

Having done all she could do for her beloved son, Hagar could not bear to sit and watch him suffer any longer. Numb with fatigue and pain, she sat down some distance away and cried as if her heart would break.

Suddenly from heaven she heard the same familiar voice she had heard in the wilderness so many years before. Once again, the Angel of the Lord asked her a question, "What is the matter, Hagar? Be not afraid. God has heard the voice of the lad where he is. Get up and support your son, for I will make a great nation of his descendants."[17]

Startled, she looked up and saw a well of fresh water only a few feet away. Struggling to her feet, she hurried over and refilled the water skin. With the water God had provided, her son drank in new life.

For the second time, Jesus Christ had visited Hagar in her misery to save her life and the life of her son. Again, there had been the promise of a hopeful future for Ishmael.

As Ishmael grew older, his mother traveled to Egypt and brought him back a wife. By this act, she proved that she was still a heathen in her heart. Her extended time around Abraham and Sarah had not completely changed that. Even the visitation by Jesus Christ had not really changed her heart. The Lord on whom she had called in her need, who had helped her, had not become the Lord of her life. He was not allowed to possess her heart.

Because the Lord knew that she would choose the idols of

her past, He had permitted her forced departure from Abraham's family. Instead of enjoying a sheltered and secure existence near Abraham, she had chosen to live a nomadic life in the desert. Because of Hagar and Ishmael's dreadful choice to assert themselves instead of living by faith in Abraham's God, the entire history of the world has been affected. Ishmael became the founder of the Arab nations, while the Israelites are the descendants of Isaac. The enmity of these two races still continues today and the Middle East situation remains extremely explosive.

Yet, in spite of everything, Hagar stands in history as a proof that Jesus Christ loves people. Every man, woman, and unborn child is loved by Him. His demonstration to Hagar proved that every person in need who calls out to Him will be answered. Jesus Christ, who was willing to reveal Himself to a woman who had reached the end of her possibilities, even now is available to everyone who seeks Him.

Hagar, whose extreme need was met by Jesus Christ
(Genesis 16:1-16; 21:1-21)

Questions:
1. Describe the story of Judges 13:3-24 briefly in your own words. What similarity do you see with Hagar?
2. The Bible tells of other appearances of the Angel of the Lord (Genesis 32:24-30; Joshua 5:13-15; Judges 6:11-24). What were the reactions of these people and in what ways are they similar to Hagar's?
3. How deeply did Jesus Christ humble Himself before men? (Philippians 2:5-11)
4. What goal did He have in mind when He came to earth?
5. What attitude should people have toward one another? (1 Peter 5:5-6) Why?
6. Have you experienced Christ's personal interest in you? If you have, give an example.

2

"The mountain ridge of Sodom consists entirely of rock salt. One of its forms remotely resembles a female figure. Tour guides still point to this as being the pillar of salt into which Lot's wife was changed."

The Author

Lot's wife, who did not take the grace of God seriously

Genesis 19:1-17 Now the two angels came to Sodom in the evening as Lot was sitting in the gate of Sodom. When Lot saw them, he rose to meet them and bowed down with his face to the ground. And he said, "Now behold, my lords, please turn aside into your servant's house, and spend the night, and wash your feet; then you may rise early and go on your way." They said however, "No, but we shall spend the night in the square." Yet he urged them strongly, so they turned aside to him and entered his house; and he prepared a feast for them, and baked unleavened bread, and they ate.

Before they lay down, the men of the city, the men of Sodom, surrounded the house, both young and old, all the people from every quarter; and they called to Lot and said to him, "Where are the men who came to you tonight? Bring them out to us that we may have relations with them." But Lot went out to them at the doorway, and shut the door behind him, and said, "Please, my brothers, do not act wickedly. Now behold, I have two daughters who have not had relations with man; please let me bring them out to you, and do to them whatever you like; only do nothing to these men,

inasmuch as they have come under the shelter of my roof."
But they said, "Stand aside." Furthermore, they said, "This
one came in as an alien, and already he is acting like a judge;
now we will treat you worse than them." So they pressed
hard against Lot and came near to break the door. But the
men reached out their hands and brought Lot into the house
with them, and shut the door. And they struck the men who
were at the doorway of the house with blindness, both small
and great, so that they wearied themselves trying to find the
doorway. Then the men said to Lot, "Whom else have you
here? A son-in-law, and your sons, and your daughters, and
whomever you have in the city, bring them out of the place;
for we are about to destroy this place, because their outcry
has become so great before the Lord that the Lord has sent
us to destroy it."
And Lot went out and spoke to his sons-in-law, who were
to marry his daughters, and said, "Up, get out of this place,
for the Lord will destroy the city." But he appeared to his
sons-in-law to be jesting. And when morning dawned, the
angels urged Lot, saying, "Up, take your wife and your two
daughters, who are here, lest you be swept away in the
punishment of the city." But he hesitated. So the men seized
his hand and the hand of his wife and the hands of his
daughters, for the compassion of the Lord was upon him;
and they brought him out, and put him outside the city. And it
came about when they had brought them outside, that one
said, "Escape for your life! Do not look behind you, and do
not stay anywhere in the valley; escape to the mountains, lest
you be swept away."

Genesis 19:24-26 Then the Lord rained on Sodom and
Gomorrah brimstone and fire from the Lord out of heaven,
and He overthrew those cities, and all the valley, and all the
inhabitants of the cities, and what grew on the ground. But
his wife, from behind him, looked back; and she became a
pillar of salt.

Nearly 20 centuries after Christ, Israeli buses arrive and
depart from the southwestern shore of the Dead Sea.
Tourists from all over the world come to see the original site

of Sodom and Gomorrah, which the Arabs still call *Bahr Loet*—"the Sea of Lot."

Not much is to be seen. Sodom is more an experience than a tourist attraction. There is no trace of life. No color brightens the landscape. The surface of the lake, about a quarter mile below sea level, is the lowest spot on earth and evaporates quickly in the nearly unbearable high temperatures. The air vibrates from the heat and is heavily laden with odors of salt and sulphur.

In this oppressive and desolate atmosphere, it does not require much imagination to realize that a catastrophe once took place here. It is as if judgment still hovers over the land. "Look, there is the wife of Lot," the tour guides say when they point to a freakish form in the rocky ridge, but that fact is difficult to substantiate.

Centuries earlier, on the other hand, this same site was pleasant, green, and full of life.[1] Business in Sodom and Gomorrah had been conducted as usual, and there was little indication that the judgment of God was coming.

Despite its peaceful surroundings, on the evening of the day God had appointed the bustling city of Sodom was in an uproar over two men who had come into town to visit Lot and his family.

Did Lot's wife know that her guests were angels sent by God to judge the city? She probably did not know how fervently the Patriarch Abraham had pleaded with God to save the cities of Sodom and Gomorrah if they had but a few righteous inhabitants.[2] "I have heard," God had said to Abraham, "that the people of Sodom and Gomorrah are utterly evil and that everything they do is wicked. I am going down to see whether these reports are true or not. Then I will know."[3]

But Lot's wife did know that life in Sodom had been immoral for years. Sodomy—an unnatural aspect of sexuality[4] —was so openly practiced that it received its name from the city of Sodom. The situation had become so bad in recent years that the male population of the town—young and old —had run out to rape her husband's guests.

---

1. Genesis 13:10
2. Genesis 18:23-33
3. Genesis 18:20-21
4. Romans 1:26-27

New Testament writers confirm the wickedness of Sodom and Gomorrah. They "indulged in gross immorality" (Jude 7) and thus were condemned and reduced to ashes (2 Peter 2:6).

She watched her husband leave the safety of their home to try to bargain with the unruly crowd, violent with passion. She became upset when Lot offered her two virgin daughters to them in exchange for the two men, but from that point on the situation began moving too quickly for her to comprehend.

First the Sodomites turned their anger against Lot so furiously that only a miracle, an intervention by the men of God themselves, saved her husband's life.

Then she listened while the two men asked Lot several serious questions. "What relatives do you have in this city?" they asked. "Sons-in-law, sons, daughters? Take them away from here! Do this as quickly as possible, for we are going to destroy the city completely. God has sent us to do this."[5]

At first she thought that the visitors were only trying to scare Lot unnecessarily. But they had saved her husband from the mob and so she began to pay more attention to their words.

Her husband, too, listened and began to obey. Excitedly he ran out the door and tried unsuccessfully to persuade his sons-in-law to flee the city with him and his family. How he pleaded with them, only to become frustrated and humiliated when their laughter echoed in his ears. They thought he was joking and looked at him as though he had lost his senses.[6]

Perhaps Lot's wife managed to get a few hours sleep before dawn while her husband was still outside. But with the first faint glow of morning, the two visitors awakened her with urgent cries. "Quick, quick, leave the city while you still can. Otherwise you will be destroyed with it," they told her husband.[7]

She looked hesitatingly around her—at her husband, at her daughters, at her home. *Why should I leave my home?* she asked herself. *Living in this city, in this house, is good, is it not? I am familiar with everything. My husband has an honorable position on the city council and my daughters are*

5. Genesis 19:12-13
6. Genesis 19:14
7. Genesis 19:15

engaged to be married. Life is taking its natural course as usual. Nothing has really changed. Why should God's judgment suddenly come on us now?

Did Lot's wife move out of Mesopotamia with Lot and his family years before? Or did Lot meet her much later in Sodom? Her background is unknown, just like her name.

Whether she was born in Sodom or not, the city now controlled her thinking. Her heart was attached to Sodom.

The Bible does not say whether or not she had a personal relationship with God. Yet because of her marriage, she had become a close relative of Abraham, whom the Bible calls "the father of all believers."[8] Abraham and Sarah lived in Hebron, which was quite near Sodom. No doubt she had met them and through them had heard about God.

Lot, her husband, also knew the Lord God. But in the proportion that he grew attached to Sodom, he increasingly turned away from Him.

At this moment of her life, God made His decision. He could not allow the wickedness of Sodom to go on any longer. He had to punish the city because of its grave and shameless sins.

In spite of His anger, God's heart was moved toward Lot's wife and her family. He wanted to save her from the claws of death which were already outstretched toward the city. He wanted to render grace to her, to offer her a favor that she didn't really deserve. He even sent His angels to her doorstep to try to save the few people who did not need to be destroyed.

In spite of this, she wavered. She wasted precious time. The angels waited impatiently for her to move but finally could not linger a moment longer. The cup of God's wrath was filled to the brim, up till the last drop. Every second they waited meant playing with their lives.

God had done everything He could to save Lot and his family. Even though Lot's love for his Lord had cooled off, God still considered him a righteous man.[9] But now the family had to listen to His messengers and take their warnings to heart. They had to leave their city of sin behind.

8. Genesis 17:4-5
9. 2 Peter 2:8

Suddenly one of the angels grasped the hand of Lot's wife and led her out the door of her own home. His voice urged her on. "Don't look back. Keep moving. Escape to the mountains, so that you won't be destroyed."[10]

Time having run out, Lot and his family left their home. When they reached the outskirts of the city, Lot asked permission to stay in the small, nearby city of Zoar. The angels granted his request, but urged him to avoid wasting any time. "Hurry, escape to Zoar," the angels stated, "for we can't do anything until you are safe."[11]

So the family left for Zoar. According to Eastern custom, Lot went first. His wife followed a few steps behind.

They had scarcely reached the little city when judgment broke loose. Sulphur and fire rained down from heaven on Sodom and Gomorrah. Nature's forces lashed the two cities violently, turning them into ashes. The entire region was wiped away from the face of the earth by the hand of God. No human being, no animal, no little blade of grass or small shrub remained alive.

"God speaks once or twice to a man, but he doesn't listen," said one of Job's friends, ". . . causing men to change their minds, . . . warning them of the penalties of sin, and keeping them from falling into a trap" (Job 33:14, 17, literally from the Dutch).

When heaven's violence burst loose, Lot's wife gave proof that she had not taken the voice of God seriously. She looked back. Her feet had stepped away from Sodom but her heart still lingered there.

That look became fatal to her. The rain of sulphur and salt overtook her, covered her, suffocated her, and became her grave. Eighteen words from the Bible describe her story. "But Lot's wife looked back as she was following along behind him and became a pillar of salt."[12]

She could have escaped death, for God had warned her in time. But she did not take His warning seriously. She ignored His grace, thus committing a grave error. To use David's words, she cared nothing for God or what He had done.[13] The words of Isaiah might also be directly applied to her. "Though the wicked is shown favor, he does not learn

10. Genesis 19:17   12. Genesis 19:26
11. Genesis 19:21-22   13. Psalm 28:5

righteousness; he deals unjustly in the land of uprightness, and does not perceive the majesty of the Lord."[14]

That negligence cost her her life. She didn't allow God to save her. She didn't accept the saving hand that He had stretched out toward her. She died because of her unwillingness to obey and act on faith, rather than because of the sins of Sodom. She had received the grace of God in vain.[15]

Jesus later used her as an example of warning. "Remember what happened to Lot's wife!" He said to His disciples, in view of the final judgment still to come.[16]

Lot's wife has passed the point of being saved. Her doom has been sealed. Yet her memory can still be a blessing if people who read her story are willing to accept the grace God is still offering. There is a fullness of grace in Jesus Christ,[17] and people who believe in Him receive grace, an undeserved gift of God.[18]

"It is a terrifying thing to fall into the hands of the living God," writes the author of Hebrews. ". . . For our God is a consuming fire" (Hebrews 10:31; 12:29).

There is hope for every human being who takes what the Bible says seriously. "So we must listen very carefully to the truths we have heard, or we may drift away from them. For since the messages from angels have always proven true and people have always been punished for disobeying them, what makes us think that we can escape if we are indifferent to this great salvation announced by the Lord Jesus Himself, and passed on to us by those who heard Him speak?"[19]

14. Isaiah 26:10   17. Ephesians 1:7-8

15. 2 Corinthians 6:1   18. Ephesians 2:8

16. Luke 17:32   19. Hebrews 2:1-3

Lot's wife, who did not take the grace of God seriously
(Genesis 19:1-17, 24-26)

Questions:
1. Summarize the story of Lot's wife briefly in your own words. (Also read Genesis 13:5-13.)
2. What was the Sodomites' major sin? (Also read Jude 7 and 2 Peter 2:6-8.)
3. What struck you in connection with the grace that God offered Lot's wife? (Also read Job 33:14, 17-18; 2 Corinthians 6:1.)
4. What do you believe to be the sin which cost Lot's wife her life?
5. Consider this story in light of Hebrews 2:1-3. What are your conclusions?
6. What principle did you learn from the example of Lot's wife and how can it influence your life favorably?

Rachel, attractive on the outside, disappointing on the inside

Genesis 29:1-30 Then Jacob went on his journey, and came to the land of the sons of the east. And he looked, and saw a well in the field, and behold, three flocks of sheep were lying there beside it, for from that well they watered the flocks. Now the stone on the mouth of the well was large. When all the flocks were gathered there, they would then roll the stone from the mouth of the well, and water the sheep, and put the stone back in its place on the mouth of the well.

And Jacob said to them, "My brothers, where are you from?" And they said, "We are from Haran." And he said to them, "Do you know Laban the son of Nahor?" And they said, "We know him." And he said to them, "Is it well with him?" And they said, "It is well, and behold, Rachel his daughter is coming with the sheep." And he said, "Behold, it is still high day; it is not time for the livestock to be gathered. Water the sheep, and go, pasture them." But they said, "We cannot, until all the flocks are gathered, and they roll the stone from the mouth of the well; then we water the sheep."

While he was still speaking with them, Rachel came with her father's sheep, for she was a shepherdess. And it came

*From *Women of the Old Testament* by Abraham Kuyper, pages 32-33. Copyright © 1933, 1961 by Zondervan Publishing House. Used by permission.

about, when Jacob saw Rachel the daughter of Laban his
mother's brother, and the sheep of Laban his mother's
brother, that Jacob went up, and rolled the stone from the
mouth of the well, and watered the flock of Laban his
mother's brother. Then Jacob kissed Rachel, and lifted his
voice and wept. And Jacob told Rachel that he was a relative
of her father and that he was Rebekah's son, and she ran
and told her father.

So it came about, when Laban heard the news of Jacob
his sister's son, that he ran to meet him, and embraced him
and kissed him, and brought him to his house. Then he
related to Laban all these things. And Laban said to him,
"Surely you are my bone and my flesh." And he stayed with
him a month. Then Laban said to Jacob, "Because you are
my relative, should you therefore serve me for nothing? Tell
me, what shall your wages be?"

Now Laban had two daughters; the name of the older was
Leah, and the name of the younger was Rachel. And Leah's
eyes were weak, but Rachel was beautiful of form and face.
Now Jacob loved Rachel, so he said, "I will serve you seven
years for your younger daughter Rachel." And Laban said,
"It is better that I give her to you than that I should give her to
another man; stay with me." So Jacob served seven years
for Rachel and they seemed to him but a few days because
of his love for her.

Then Jacob said to Laban, "Give me my wife, for my time
is completed, that I may go in to her." And Laban gathered
all the men of the place, and made a feast. Now it came
about in the evening that he took his daughter Leah, and
brought her to him; and Jacob went in to her. Laban also
gave his maid Zilpah to his daughter Leah as a maid.

So it came about in the morning that, behold, it was Leah!
And he said to Laban, "What is this you have done to me?
Was it not for Rachel that I served with you? Why then have
you deceived me?" But Laban said, "It is not the practice in
our place, to marry off the younger before the first-born.
Complete the bridal week of this one, and we will give you
the other also for the service which you shall serve with me
for another seven years." And Jacob did so and completed
her week, and he gave him his daughter Rachel as his wife.
Laban also gave his maid Bilhah to his daughter Rachel as

her maid. So Jacob went in to Rachel also, and indeed he loved Rachel more than Leah, and he served with Laban for another seven years.

(Also read Genesis 30—33; 35.)

Somewhat confused, Rachel glanced at the foreigner who stood next to the well. She had met him only minutes before when, according to her daily routine, she had driven her sheep there for a drink. As she neared the well, she watched in amazement as the stranger singlehandedly rolled the heavy stone from its mouth with ease. The job usually required the strength of several strong men.

Even though she had never seen the man before, he did not appear a total stranger to her. Something about him was familiar. Moments later she understood why; he introduced himself as her cousin. He was Jacob, the son of Rebekah, her aunt, who had moved years ago from her home to Canaan in order to marry Isaac, his father.

He thinks that I'm beautiful, she thought as she stealthily observed the way in which he looked at her. This thought was nothing new to Rachel. She was used to attracting attention with her pretty face and lovely figure and had learned to accept the homage paid her beauty matter-of-factly, like many beautiful women have learned to do. But the way this man was looking at her was different. His penetrating eyes contained a sparkle of awakening love, and his kiss of greeting had seemed to mean more than an impetuous greeting of a newly arrived relative.

Captivated by Rachel's beauty from the first moment he saw her, Jacob did have a deep and growing love for his pretty cousin. He demonstrated his interest in her a month later by becoming a member of her father's household.

"You are a relative, all right, but that doesn't mean that you have to work for me without pay," Laban said to Jacob. "How much do you want to earn? Just name your price."[1]

---

1. Genesis 29:15

No hesitation rang in Jacob's answer. "I will serve you seven years for your younger daughter Rachel," he said resolutely.[2] He loved Rachel and was willing to do much in order to get her as his wife. Although seven years was a long time, for Jacob the many weeks and months seemed to dwindle into just a few days because of his tremendous love for Rachel.

And Rachel? What were her feelings during this time? Did she love Jacob in the way that he loved her? The Bible does not tell us about her feelings nor about her reaction to the terrible event that occurred at her wedding, although it must have been utterly painful to her.

Laban, thinking about what suited him best, did not mind using crooked means to reach his goal. He deliberately took advantage of Jacob's passionate love for Rachel in order to marry off his unattractive and older daughter, Leah, first. By exchanging his daughters, Laban tricked Jacob into marrying Leah instead of Rachel.

Jacob expressed his anger about Laban's deception in harsh words the following morning, but there is no record of Rachel's reaction. Hadn't she longed those seven long years for him just like he had longed for her? Did the exchange of the brides bring sorrow to her heart? What were her inner thoughts? Was her outward beauty a resemblance of the beauty of her heart? Her reactions to the circumstances of her life provide the answers.

A week after the wedding, Jacob was married again, this time to Rachel, on the condition that he would serve Laban seven more years.

A marriage of one man with two women had special problems which were even more intensified since the women were sisters. Thus Rachel and Leah did not escape the tensions accompanying such an undesirable situation, and the fact that Jacob loved Rachel and not Leah made matters worse.

Leah, who experienced the pain of living with a husband who didn't love her, took her need to God. God, in turn, rewarded her with six sons and a daughter. Deprived of outward beauty, Leah's inward beauty grew under pressure and she showed a reverence for God.

Rachel, on the other hand, reacted differently, pitifully. Her character left little room for gratitude and empathy. Jealous of Leah, she thought only of herself. To her, it was a matter of fact that she was privileged above Leah, that Jacob loved her, and that she was attractive. Yet, concentrating her thoughts on the children she missed, Rachel begrudged Leah her motherly happiness. In her heart, Rachel refused to accept the fact that she lagged behind her sister at this point.

"Give me children!" she exclaimed to Jacob bitterly. "Otherwise I'd rather be dead."[3] These heartless words rudely revealed the place that Jacob held in her heart. She preferred death over her shame. Jacob apparently was not worth much to her.

Her exclamation also dishonored God. Although Jacob pointed out that Rachel addressed her complaint to the wrong person—God alone gives or keeps the blessing of children—he could not convince his wife.

The pain of unfulfilled desire did not drive Rachel to God. Instead, she initiated her own forced solution. "Take my servant-girl Bilhah as your wife," she advised Jacob. "Her children will then be counted as mine."[4] She was aware of the old custom which would allow Bilhah's children to be legally regarded as hers and thus Jacob's true offspring.

When Bilhah's son was born, the event gave even deeper insight into Rachel's character. "God has given me justice," she said, and then named the baby Dan.[5]

Although she mentioned the name of God, it is evident that for Rachel the child was part of her competition with Leah. Rachel had claimed her rights; having lagged behind her sister in childbirth, she wanted to change her status.

This thought became even clearer when Bilhah's second son, Naphtali, was born. His name meant "wrestling," and represented what Rachel felt was a growing victory in the fierce contest with her sister. Rachel was being motivated

3. Genesis 30:1
4. Genesis 30:3
5. Genesis 30:6

by bitterness, a dangerous and infectious attitude that has always affected people and their environments negatively.[6]

When Rachel brought a concubine into the marriage, she started a dangerous chain reaction. Before long, Leah did the same with her servant-girl Zilpah. At this point—as if problems were not big enough already—the family consisted of one man with four wives.

How deeply Rachel was touched in her soul by her husband's love remains unclear in Scripture. But it is evident that she manipulated his love in her competition with Leah. As the years passed, her jealousy remained. She did not give room to feelings of sympathy for her sister, who kept hoping to win Jacob's love. The words "give me" were uppermost in her thoughts.

A day during the wheat harvest revealed Rachel's selfish attitude. Noticing that Reuben, Leah's first son, had brought his mother some fruit, Rachel wanted some too. Mandrakes were believed to stimulate the power to love. They were scarce and thus Reuben's find was rare. "Give me some of your son's mandrakes," she urged. "Then Jacob may sleep with you tonight."[7] Condescendingly, Rachel distributed love like merchandise in order to please herself. Keeping the reins of the family and her husband in her hands, Rachel proudly manipulated to gain her own ends.

Apparently she did not know the real meaning of the word *love*. The vibrating warmth that could have been an outflow of love seemed foreign to her. What she knew best of all was self-love. The outward beauty which made her attractive made a painful contradiction when placed against her inner hardness and pride. Rachel's interest was frozen into a chilling circle around her own person.

When the real issues and values of life are compared, Rachel lagged behind Leah, whose life was controlled by God to a much greater degree. But that didn't prevent God from extending His goodness toward Rachel. Miserable human egotism could not curtail the grace of God. The Lord saw Rachel's struggle. Knowing her passionate desire

6. Hebrews 12:15
7. Genesis 30:14-15

for a child of her own, He gave her a son, Joseph. When she named him, she proved once again how deep-seated her feelings of lagging behind her sister were.

"God has removed the dark slur against my name," she remarked. She then continued, "May I also have another."[8] Rachel remained the same old Rachel, even after her own son was born. Her thoughts remained egotistical, jealous, and ungrateful. "Give me, give me," was still her repeated life-song. Her spirit of competition choked her gratitude, for those two attitudes could not live in her heart at the same time.

Yet something in the patriarchal home changed after Joseph's birth. What the children of Jacob's other wives could not do, the son of beloved Rachel did. Jacob became homesick for his father's land. After 14 years of toil, he lost his willingness to work on foreign soil for someone else. Although his father-in-law convinced him to stay a little longer in Haran, Jacob started building the future of his own tribe. After six additional years of hard work—during which he became rich—he decided definitely to return to Canaan.

On that day, Jacob called Rachel and Leah to his side. He explained to them how the Lord God had commanded him to start the journey back to his homeland. Both wives agreed with his decision. "Do as God has told you," they answered unanimously.[9] Both women would gladly go with him. There was no conflict over his decision.

It is remarkable to see, however, how one single occurrence could reveal the inward being of a person so sharply. Special circumstances that interrupt a person's daily routine have the tendency to strip him of all the fringes with which he has adorned himself for years.

A change of this sort affected Rachel as she prepared for the long trek to Canaan. Naturally, such a trip was a big step for a young Eastern woman who had never left the boundaries of her village. The journey would be long and the future country was unknown.

The fact that God had given Jacob the call to depart and

8. Genesis 30:23-24
9. Genesis 31:14-16$

the encouraging assurance of His nearness proved to be no guarantee for Rachel. Many years of being married to Jacob apparently had not brought her nearer to his God.

Obviously her husband's love had given Rachel little inspiration to get to know him very well. His deepest thoughts remained foreign to her and she didn't share his spiritual life. Although Jacob's character did have some striking flaws—his manipulation of business deals and his deceit—his faith in God always triumphed.

As Rachel's long-standing securities began to fail her, she clung to something she could hold onto—the household idols of her father. While Jacob was on his way to renew a covenant with God, Rachel was seeking refuge in pagan images.

Leah, who also had been born and educated in this land where idols were served, had developed a growing confidence in God instead. She, unlike Rachel, had grown to trust the God of her husband, Jacob.

While the large family prepared to leave in secret, accompanied by the animal herds, Rachel stole her father's idols. This act shed even more light on her relationship with Jacob, for she committed the theft without telling him. She did not share her burdens with him. In spite of Jacob's great love for Rachel, husband and wife never achieved real closeness and communication in their married life.

By stealing the idols, Rachel risked her life. Jacob was so insulted when Laban accused him of having stolen his household gods that he raged, "A curse upon anyone who took them. He will not live!"[10]

Rachel then used a lie to escape death. Seated on her camel saddle under which she had hidden the idols, she found a clever, acceptable excuse. Pretending indisposition because she was a woman, she did not leave her seat when Laban searched her tent. Thus Laban was unable to find the idols. Rachel's deception remained undetected, but her deed and the stolen images defiled the religion of the family of the Patriarch Jacob. Later the harmful results of her act would be seen.

10. Genesis 31:32

The Bible is not vague about God's view of the human heart. It clearly describes the heart in many different chapters. The human heart is bent toward evil "from its youth."[11] The heart is so deceitful, sick, and complicated that only God really knows it.[12] He calls it proud and stubborn [13] and says that those who are "proud in heart" are disgusting.[14] Truly God will not tolerate a sinful, unclean heart.

The human being is unable to change his own heart. No matter how much effort is expended, he cannot reform it himself. Only God can transform it. Therefore He invites everyone to "Give me your heart,"[15] to allow Him to work.

Yet, in spite of His love, God often allows people to suffer in order to change their stubborn, self-willed hearts and bend them toward Him. He tests men and women to see if they are prepared to do His will.[16]

David, Israel's greatest king, later expressed an understanding of these facts when he prayed, "Create in me a clean heart, O God" (Psalm 51:10).

In light of these facts, Rachel's heart was not exceptionally bad or unusually self-willed. Instead of surrendering her life to God, she chose to govern her own life. That wrong decision of self-rule led to egotism, and multiplied her personal problems.

Since God's love did not have the chance to light her heart through, it remained blocked up in darkness and the cold of pride and could hardly release warmth. When a human being wants to share his heart with others, he first has to surrender his heart to God. Only then does he receive and pass on God's love, the warmth of which enables his life to become sparkling, happy, and warm.

Rachel's frustration to prove herself in motherhood led to her death. Before Jacob and his family definitely settled in the Promised Land, Rachel died in childbirth. With her last breath, Rachel named her baby son Ben-oni, which meant "son of my sorrow." But Jacob later renamed the baby Benjamin, "son of my right hand."

In spite of the seriousness and unhappiness of Rachel's person, a ray of hope still existed in her older son, Joseph. He was still young when his mother died, but he grew up to

11. Genesis 8:21
12. Jeremiah 17:9-10
13. Jeremiah 5:23
14. Proverbs 16:5
15. Proverbs 23:26
16. Deuteronomy 8:2, 16

be an exceptional man of God in whose life God had absolute preeminence. He was destined to become an extraordinary blessing to the Hebrew people.

Shortly before Rachel died, Jacob renewed his covenant with God. He removed all foreign idols from his household and buried them. After this purification had taken place, God so closely aligned Himself with Jacob and his family that all his neighbors were deeply impressed. Despite all the past mistakes, a new beginning with God had taken place.

Did Rachel's heart go out to God in the last phase of her life? Did the motherless boy, Joseph, become the product of his father's education? Or had Rachel changed enough through God's power that she was able to make an indelible impression upon him?

Whatever the answers, Rachel's pitiful and unfulfilled life could have been exciting and full of meaning if only her inner beauty had matched her lovely outward appearance.

Rachel, attractive on the outside, disappointing on the inside (Genesis 29:1-30; also read Genesis 30—33; 35.)

Questions:
1. Write out what you learned about the human heart.
2. What does the Bible reveal about the heart of Rachel?
3. What do you consider to be her most striking characteristic?
4. In what ways could Rachel's life have had a more positive influence?
5 Do you see any blessings that resulted from Rachel's life? If so, name them.
6. With what you learned about Rachel, can you help yourself or people around you? In what ways?

4

*"This polygamous family, with many shameful things to their credit, was accepted of God, as a whole, to be the beginning of the Twelve Tribes which became the Messianic Nation, chosen of God to bring the Savior into the world. This shows that God uses human beings as they are."**
Henry H. Halley

Leah, a woman whose unhappy marriage became God's blessing to humanity

Genesis 29:21-35 Then Jacob said to Laban, "Give me my wife, for my time is completed, that I may go in to her." And Laban gathered all the men of the place, and made a feast. Now it came about in the evening that he took his daughter Leah, and brought her to him; and Jacob went in to her. Laban also gave his maid Zilpah to his daughter Leah as a maid.

So it came about in the morning that, behold, it was Leah! And he said to Laban, "What is this you have done to me? Was it not for Rachel that I served with you? Why then have you deceived me?" But Laban said, "It is not the practice in our place, to marry off the younger before the first-born. Complete the bridal week of this one, and we will give you the other also for the service which you shall serve with me for another seven years." And Jacob did so and completed her week, and he [Laban] gave him his daughter Rachel as his wife. Laban also gave his maid Bilhah to his daughter Rachel as her maid. So Jacob went in to Rachel also, and indeed he loved Rachel more than Leah, and he served with Laban for another seven years.

* *Halley's Bible Handbook*, page 104. Copyright © 1965 by Halley's Bible Handbook, Inc. Reprinted by permission.

Now the Lord saw that Leah was unloved, and He opened her womb, but Rachel was barren. And Leah conceived and bore a son and named him Reuben, for she said, "Because the Lord has seen my affliction; surely now my husband will love me." Then she conceived again and bore a son and said, "Because the Lord has heard that I am unloved, He has therefore given me this son also." So she named him Simeon. And she conceived again and bore a son and said, "Now this time my husband will become attached to me, because I have borne him three sons." Therefore he was named Levi. And she conceived again and bore a son and said, "This time I will praise the Lord." Therefore she named him Judah. Then she stopped bearing.

(Also read the Scripture portions under Rachel.)

Leah's illusions had fallen to pieces, totally broken. The few hours of darkness which now lay behind her had been the happiest of her life. Hoping against hope, she had lain quietly, savoring what she knew might be short-lived happiness. While she surrendered herself to the love of her bridegroom, at the same time she dreaded the hour of truth. She feared the break of day.

The hour came slowly; the first sunbeam striped the earthen tent floor. Then her bridegroom woke up and saw her, his bride. The disappointment she had anticipated—she had not had enough courage to prepare him—darted across his face. Her husband Jacob expected her sister Rachel to be beside him, the woman he had loved from the very first moment he had seen her seven long years ago. For Rachel he had worked, had hoped, and had dreamed. With Rachel he had expected to pass his night after the wedding. Jacob had thought of only one woman—Rachel.

He looked sleepily at Leah and then screamed as the truth rudely awakened him. Bewildered, desperate, he leaped to his feet, wondering how such a dreadful lot could have befallen him. Slowly his confusion turned to fury as he realized that he had been deceived. Under cover of the night and the bride's veil, the wrong girl had been brought to his tent because of financial and social implications.

Leah no doubt understood Jacob's sense of betrayal. He had been treated as one not yet of age or wise. He had been tricked like a being void of reason, a pawn of another's authority. A woman whom he did not love had been forced on him. As these and other thoughts cut through his being, Jacob's reaction made it utterly clear that there was no place for Leah in his heart. She meant nothing to him, even though she cared for him deeply.

There is no turning back, Leah thought to herself. *In spite of everything, I am his wife. My future has been decided. I am married to a man who doesn't care about me in the least.* While she reasoned to herself, Jacob stormed out of the tent. He had to find Laban, his father-in-law, who had treated him so poorly.

Leah remained in the tent alone, continuing the dialogue of her thoughts. The future looked gloomy. But hope still existed because she loved Jacob. She simply would not and could not believe that her cause was lost. *Perhaps,* she reasoned, *the future will reveal itself brighter than it looks right now. Maybe Jacob will change his mind after he sees how much I love him. Maybe everything will turn out all right when I give him a son. Maybe, maybe . . .*

In the meantime, Jacob faced Laban, restrained fury and accusation in his voice. "What a rotten thing you have done to me," he raged. "I have served you seven years for Rachel. Why have you deceived me?"[1]

Laban turned slowly, looking down at his feet. His defense was weak, his excuse poor. "It is customary in our country that the eldest daughter marries first, then the youngest," he answered, ignoring the fact that this was an objection he should have raised earlier.[2] The plain fact was that he had calculated the advantages he would have in such a dishonest venture. Through deceit, he had ensnared his hard-working son-in-law and now would have cheap labor even longer. This way, the groom had to pay a high bridal price. At the same time, Laban had also given his eldest

1. Genesis 29:25
2. Genesis 29:26

daughter in marriage. She was not as pretty as Rachel and probably had been passed over by prospective suitors.

Jacob had little choice. The only thing he could do was to agree with Laban's proposal to marry Rachel also, as soon as the seven-day wedding feast was over. That decision obliged him to serve his father-in-law for another seven years.

But Jacob also allowed his thoughts to wander back to his parental home. Long ago he had cheated his father in a similar way by changing persons with his brother. He, the youngest son, had stolen the blessing which belonged to his brother Esau.[3] The deceiver had been deceived, defeated with his own weapon. He now suffered the same sorrow he had inflicted upon others.

Thus Leah began her first days of married life, the only days that she had her husband to herself. The man who in his thoughts was already with another woman could not wait to call that woman his own. Leah craved a love which she did not receive. Would she ever receive it?

God knows every deed that we do and often allows its consequences to take place. "Do not be deceived, God is not mocked; for whatever a man sows, this he will also reap" (Galatians 6:7).

Her marriage showed little resemblance to the covenant between the partners God had in mind when he created man and woman for one another. God's plan for marriage was monogamy, the coming together of one man with one woman.[4]

The Israelites, however, disobeyed God and began to take other wives like the heathen around them. Although God tolerated this, He also knew that no man could violate His order of creation without paying for it. That pain is what Leah experienced. She tasted the bitter fruit of polygamy—wedlock of one man with more than one woman—every day of her life.

As the years passed since that first wedding night, the door to her husband's heart remained tightly closed for Leah. Part of this was due to her looks; she couldn't compare in physical beauty with her sister. Her eyes, for exam-

---

3. Genesis 27:5-40
4. Genesis 1:27; 2:24

ple, were tender and weak but the exact nature of the problem is unknown. Did she, like so many in her country, suffer from an eye disease that made her looks offensive? Was she cross-eyed? Were her eyes healthy but lacking the color and sparkle that made other Eastern beauties so attractive? Were they a pale blue instead of a shining brown?

Although handicapped in this one important area of her life, Leah nevertheless was blessed by God in a special way. "God never closes a door unless He opens another," states an old proverb. For Leah, this was the door to motherhood. "Because Jacob was slighting Leah," the Bible reads, "Jehovah let her have a child."[5]

The marriage relationship is so exclusive, so holy, that God used it in the Old Testament as a symbol of the relationship between Himself and His people (Hosea 2:19), and between Christ and His church (Ephesians 5:28-32). He expects a lifelong faithfulness between the marriage partners (Malachi 2:14-16) which will lead to happiness (Ecclesiastes 9:9). The ideal woman praised by Solomon also functions within a monogamous marriage framework (Proverbs 31:10-31).

God was not hindered by the fact that Leah was not attractive. He did not judge her by her outward appearance. He looked at her heart, which was going out toward Him.[6] Rachel's heart, on the other hand, was rapidly becoming selfish and self-centered.

Sorrow often brings with it a hidden danger. It can make a person self-centered, shutting him off from fellowmen, the outside world, and from God. In Leah's life, though, the opposite was true. Her sorrow drove her to God. This is seen in the names of her sons.

She named her firstborn Reuben, which meant "He has seen my affliction." Her thought behind this name was that God had noticed her trouble. She knew that anyone could trust God with great confidence. Hadn't God promised that if someone called on Him, He would answer and also show that person His salvation?[7] Leah, who had experienced God's faithfulness and love, expressed that certainty at the birth of her second son, Simeon. "Cast your burden on the Lord, and He will sustain you," the Psalmist David would sing centuries later.[8] "When I am afraid, I will put my trust in Thee."[9]

5. Genesis 29:31
6. 1 Samuel 16:7
7. Psalm 91:15-16
8. Psalm 55:22
9. Psalm 56:3

That name meant "The Lord has heard." As often as she mentioned the name Simeon, she reminded herself and those around her of God's goodness. Leah shared her problems with God and did not forget to honor Him openly after He answered her prayers, something that He expected from the people.[10]

The 12 tribes of Israel—named after Jacob's sons—would refer to God's faithfulness until the end of human history. A tremendous heritage would come through Leah, the woman with the unhappy marriage. Sorrow in Leah's life was God's instrument; it caused her to become a building-stone of the house of Israel. Later generations would praise her for that.[11]

The natural longing after her husband's love—it could not be otherwise—remained. But the absence of it brought Leah to a greater understanding of God. Her life was enriched by her sorrow, ripened by testing. Her confidence in God grew.

When her fourth son, Judah, was born, the love for God in Leah's heart was stronger than her love for Jacob. "This time I will praise the Lord," she exclaimed jubilantly.[12] For the first time, she did not mention the love of her husband. She was not aware of the prophetic meaning of this moment. She didn't know that with Judah's birth a new era was beginning. From the descendants of this son, out of the tribe of Judah the Messiah would come. Every generation would praise the name of Judah.

Leah would never know how privileged she was. This fact would only be revealed many centuries later. Leah was used by God to be a blessing to all humanity. Indeed, through her the birth of the Saviour of the world—Jesus Christ—came nearer.

Meanwhile, her life didn't proceed without tensions. Again and again Leah gave herself to a husband who didn't love her. For Leah, the joy of coming together as marriage partners had a bitter taste. With unfailing intuition, she sensed that her surrender of love did not set Jacob's heart aflame. The marriage act performed in this way was

10. Psalm 50:15
11. Ruth 4:11
12. Genesis 29:35

humiliating to her. It became an insult. Yet the strange fact remained that while Jacob loved Rachel, Leah gave birth to his children.

Contrary to other women of the Bible,[13] Leah did not become proud when Rachel remained childless. She remained open and humble despite her sister's envy. Yet the atmosphere in the family remained heavy and explosive. Little incidents revealed how touchy the situation was. One day, for example, Reuben wanted to surprise his mother with mandrakes—small prune-like fruits also called "love apples." Some people of that day believed that the mandrakes caused riches, happiness, and even fertility. Envious of the attention Leah received from her son, Rachel wanted some mandrakes. "Give me some of them," she demanded.[14]

Her demands led to a strong argument in which Leah also lost her composure. "Wasn't it enough to steal my husband?" she replied sharply. "And now you will steal my son's mandrakes too?"[15]

Rachel knew how to get what she wanted. "Jacob will sleep with you tonight because of the mandrakes," she promised.[16] Rachel, the younger of the two sisters and the second wife, extended her favors to Leah in a superior way.

It was an unworthy proposal in light of the holiness of wedlock and basic principles of human rights. Yet Leah accepted the bullying by her sister. The woman who was willing to do everything she could to win her husband's love humiliated herself, once again.

When Jacob returned home from work that evening, Leah was waiting for him. Like a dog begging for the favor of his master, Leah hankered after Jacob's affection. "Please, sleep with me tonight," she begged, "for I have honestly hired you."[17] It was a miracle that the holy God still accepted people who made such a mockery of things He considered holy. Marriage and love had to be treated with respect.

Leah rapidly gave birth to two more sons, Issachar and Zebulun. Both names again resounded the love of God.

13. Genesis 16:4-5; 1 Samuel 1:2-7
14. Genesis 30:14 16. Genesis 30:15
15. Genesis 30:15 17. Genesis 30:16

Leah also became the only one of Jacob's wives to give him a daughter, Dinah.

By this time, Jacob was not only married to Leah and Rachel but to the two maids as well. The struggle to become the best had brought Rachel to offer her servant-girl to her husband. Leah, who did not want to be left behind, did the same. Those two women—Bilhah and Zilpah—increased the family with two sons each.

In spite of the unworthy manner with which this marriage was treated, the quick expansion of the family fit into God's plan. The promise He had given to Jacob's father, Abraham—that he would become a great nation—had to be fulfilled.[18] It was also God's promise to Jacob.[19]

Leah, with her deep-seated faith, had a prominent place in that plan. She brought six of the twelve sons—heads of tribes—into the world. But her life didn't become any easier. She never won Jacob's love. As long as she lived, Jacob always preferred Rachel.

Leah experienced this partiality again when the family returned to the Promised Land. As they neared the border, Jacob became afraid of his brother Esau, whom he had tricked 20 years before and from whose wrath he had fled the county.[20] Scared of what his revengeful brother might do to his entire family, he divided it into small groups. First came his concubines and their sons. Then Leah and her children followed the first group. The most protected places in the rear were reserved for Joseph and Rachel. Rachel was farthest from the threatening danger.

Leah, the woman with the weak eyes, is recorded in history as the woman with the unhappy marriage. The Bible does not say whether Jacob refused her only because of her appearance. Maybe her disposition and character differed so much from those of her husband that harmonious unity was never formed. One thing is certain, however. Leah wept many bitter tears during her lifetime.

Shortly before his death, Jacob met with Joseph and during that meeting described how he had buried Rachel near Ephrath in Canaan.[21] Then Jacob called his sons together to

18. Genesis 12:2
19. Genesis 28:14-15
20. Genesis 27
21. Genesis 48:7

foretell their futures and told them that Leah had been buried in the family's burial cave at Machpelah. Thus Leah, after her death, was placed with honor alongside Abraham, Sarah, Isaac, and Rebekah.[22]

Leah's story is both a warning and an encouragement. Her life stands as a warning for people not to make decisions against the will of God. She also brings to a standstill those people who *In the mosque above Leah's grave in Hebron, wailing women still bewail her loudly today—nearly 4,000 years later.* try to treat love lightly or who expect to win the love of a life partner after the wedding vows have been exchanged.

The story of Leah serves as an encouragement because it gives us further insight into how God looks at a person. He based His evaluation of Leah on her heart and not on her appearance. He also accepted her in the situation as it appeared to Him. Through His love, He can and will transform a person with a nearly unbearable life burden into a channel through whom His blessings for humanity can flow. In spite of everything, Leah's place in history is honorable.

Leah, a woman whose unhappy marriage became God's blessing to humanity
(Genesis 29:21-35; also read the Scripture portions under Rachel.)

Questions:
1. What struck you most about Leah's life?
2. How would you have responded to the problems she had to face?
3. Using a Bible dictionary or encyclopedia, list the names of Leah's sons and their meanings. What impresses you most as you consider these meanings?
4. What warnings do you draw from Leah's life?
5. What encouragement do you draw from Leah's life?
6. What practical influence can Leah's life have on your own?

22. Genesis 49:30-31

5

*"There is an alarming increase in the number of
girls who, anxious for change and wanting to see
something of the world, turn aside from the shelter
of a good home and are never heard of again. Many
of them end up in sin, crime and degradation."**

Herbert Lockyer

Dinah,
a girl whose curiosity led to crime
and mourning

Genesis 34:1-15 Now Dinah the daughter of Leah, whom she
had borne to Jacob, went out to visit the daughters of the
land. And when Shechem the son of Hamor the Hivite, the
prince of the land, saw her, he took her and lay with her by
force. And he was deeply attracted to Dinah the daughter of
Jacob, and he loved the girl and spoke tenderly to her. So
Shechem spoke to his father Hamor, saying, "Get me this
young girl for a wife."

Now Jacob heard that he had defiled Dinah his daughter;
but his sons were with his livestock in the field, so Jacob kept
silent until they came in. Then Hamor the father of Shechem
went out to Jacob to speak with him. Now the sons of Jacob
came in from the field when they heard it; and the men were
grieved, and they were very angry because he had done a
disgraceful thing in Israel by lying with Jacob's daughter, for
such a thing ought not to be done.

But Hamor spoke with them, saying, "The soul of my son
Shechem longs for your daughter; please give her to him in
marriage. And intermarry with us; give your daughters to us,
and take our daughters for yourselves. Thus you shall live

*From *The Women of the Bible* by Herbert Lockyer, page 46. Copyright © 1967
by Zondervan Publishing House. Used by permission.

with us, and the land shall be open before you; live and trade in it, and acquire property in it." Shechem also said to her father and to her brothers, "If I find favor in your sight, then I will give whatever you say to me. Ask me ever so much bridal payment and gift, and I will give according as you say to me; but give me the girl in marriage."

But Jacob's sons answered Shechem and his father Hamor, with deceit, and spoke to them, because he had defiled Dinah their sister. And they said to them, "We cannot do this thing, to give our sister to one who is uncircumcised, for that would be a disgrace to us. Only on this condition will we consent to you: if you will become like us, in that every male of you be circumcised."

Genesis 34:24-29 And all who went out of the gate of his city listened to Hamor and to his son Shechem, and every male was circumcised, all who went out of the gate of his city. Now it came about on the third day, when they were in pain, that two of Jacob's sons, Simeon and Levi, Dinah's brothers, each took his sword and came upon the city unawares, and killed every male. And they killed Hamor and his son Shechem with the edge of the sword, and took Dinah from Shechem's house, and went forth. Jacob's sons came upon the slain and looted the city, because they had defiled their sister. They took their flocks and their herds and their donkeys, and that which was in the city and that which was in the field; and they captured and looted all their wealth and all their little ones and their wives, even all that was in the houses.

Dinah, the daughter of Jacob, felt bored and she had good reason to be. Life in a goatskin tent did not offer much attraction for a girl in her teens, especially since her parents were aged and she had only brothers with whom to talk.

Dinah had not had much of a chance to relax. Her life had been nomadic, constantly on the move. Originally migrating from the city of Haran in Mesopotamia[1]—about 400 miles to the northeast—her family continued to wander. Again and again after her family halted for a while, the

---

1. Genesis 31:18

tent pins would be taken out of the ground and on they would go. They would be on the move once more, moving step by step to keep pace with the animals.

Then they arrived in Canaan. Her father pitched their tents near Shalem, which belonged to the city of Shechem, and bought a piece of land.[2] Apparently he wanted to settle in the land God had promised to his forefathers Abraham and Isaac, for through the promise the land was also his.

It was remarkable, however, that Jacob did not travel several more miles to Bethel. There he had made a promise to God some 30 years earlier, shortly before he moved out of Canaan.[3] Had his love for God cooled off?

Shechem was situated in the strategic pass which cut through the Ebal, Ephraim, and Gerizim Mountains and controlled the roads to the north and the west. Boasting a beautiful location and advanced culture, Shechem was never dull. Daily the merchants and migrants who traveled from the East to Egypt passed through the city in exotic dress.

Dinah was bored of being alone. She was restless. She longed for something happier, brighter than the tents of her father. She wanted to meet other girls and had heard that the girls of Shechem offered a colorful picture because of their beautiful, Eastern costumes. Desiring to see these costumes for herself, she left the parental tent and began walking toward Shechem.

Did her parents know that Dinah was leaving? Was there no one to warn her? Hadn't her mother or father pointed out the possible dangers threatening her? In the past, Great-grandmother Sarah and Grandmother Rebekah had found themselves in great trouble when they had drawn much attention from the kings of the lands they had visited.[4] Only an intervention by God and the presence of their husbands had kept them from disaster. But Dinah was alone, young, and inexperienced.

So she arrived at Shechem. How many, if any, of the local beauties she saw is unknown. But she did end up in the bedroom of the prince of the land. Prince Shechem, the son

2. Genesis 33:18-20
3. Genesis 28:19-22; 31:13
4. Genesis 12:14-20; 26:7-11

of Hamor, saw her, took her, and raped her.

Whether Dinah consented to enter the palace or whether she did everything within her power to prevent it remains a secret. Yet within those walls she lost her purity, her virginity. Like every other girl who has shared that experience, she lost something very precious, something that could never be returned.

Her little trip launched out in curiosity and impulse set off a chain reaction of misery that ended with crime and mourning. The great sorrow that Dinah unleashed was terribly great and could not be reversed after it was set in motion.

This situation was even more serious than it first appeared. Dinah was a member of a family that had made a covenant with God. She should have been more careful, not only because of herself but also because her family represented the tribe of God's people.

While Dinah remained in the royal palace with Shechem, whose name was identical with that of the city, Jacob and his sons heard what had happened. King Hamor, Shechem's father, anticipated Jacob's response and visited him. "My son is truly in love with your daughter," he said. "Please let him marry her."[5]

Then Shechem himself arrived. A heathen prince, he had not been taught to consider God in his plans. Although he had acted wrongly with Dinah, no one could doubt his serious plans with her. His people loved him; he was very popular. "Please be kind to me," he begged. "Give your consent that she will become my wife. As far as the dowry is concerned, you name it. I will pay what you ask."[6] It was clear that Shechem felt very attached to Dinah. He loved her. And she? She was not closed to his love; she liked the way he talked to her.

In order to please her family as much as possible, Hamor suggested that Jacob and his tribe make a covenant with the people of Shechem so that they could intermarry and do business together. But Simeon and Levi, Dinah's brothers, were justifiably furious. The brothers belonged to a tribe

5. Genesis 34:8
6. Genesis 34:11-12

that had made a covenant with God and therefore had to meet higher demands. Their God expected them to be a holy people. They had to refrain from the heathen practices all around them. Under their existing law, the loss of a girl's virginity was considered a flagrant crime.[7] They were too shocked and angry to overlook the insult, for it was an outrage against all of them. "You can't do such a thing!" they raged.

Using Moses as His spokesman, God promised later Israelites that He would continue to bless them as long as they obeyed Him and kept His commandments (Exodus 19:5-6, 20).

Their fury was justified, but the way they took their revenge was not. Rather than acting honestly, Simeon and Levi moved hypocritically. Pretending to agree with King Hamor's proposal to merge the two groups of people, they set forth the condition that every male inhabitant of Shechem would have to undergo circumcision, the ritual obligatory for the Hebrew men. Their request revealed how superficially the two brothers thought about religion. They mistook its true meaning with its outward sign. And, what was far worse, they used religion to cover up premeditated murder.

After Hamor and Shechem convinced their subjects of the reasonableness of the Hebrews' request, the ceremony took place. Simeon and Levi then entered the city on the third day armed with swords. While the entire male population was in pain, unable to move because of their wounds, Simeon and Levi killed every man in the city. With their swords, they beheaded or stabbed man after man. They didn't hesitate even to slaughter Hamor and Shechem, men with whom they had pretended to discuss the covenant only a few days before. What began with the passion of lustful sensuality ended up becoming murder.

Simeon and Levi's gruesome murder of unsuspecting people wasn't even enough to cool their hatred. They also plundered the city, seizing all the flocks and herds and capturing the women and children as their prey.

The innocent-looking little trip of Dinah's had led her brothers to commit a deed that had no relation to the wrong

---

7. Deuteronomy 22:20-21

Prince Shechem had committed. Simeon and Levi had become murderers, abhorred by the world. They had cast a blame upon themselves that could never be removed. Countless men died because of their cruelty; wives and children became widows and homeless orphans who could call sorrow their only personal possession.

Through these circumstances, not only the reputations of Dinah and her brothers were disgraced; their father also suffered.

"You have made me stink among all the people of this land," he lamented. "We are so few that they will come and crush us and we will all be killed."[8]

It was in fact God's name—so closely connected with Jacob's name and that of His people[9]—that really suffered. Jacob neglected to mention this. Was it possible that he was more concerned with his own name, the talk that went on behind his back, than the honor of God? Was this temporary weakness of the father the cause of the misbehavior of his children?

His attitude toward his family was not impressive either. He rebuked Simeon and Levi about the way they had brought disgrace to him, but he did not mention their sin against God and their fellowmen.

The Bible doesn't even mention Jacob's fatherly concern and authority concerning Dinah. She didn't receive the attention from him that she needed in this painful situation. Even the love that is shown in a rebuke seemed to be kept from her.[10] Jacob was only thinking about himself.

Whether or not Dinah's mother understood and comforted her is not recorded. Yet, who else but Leah—who had suffered so much from love herself—could have been more understanding of her daughter's pain? Dinah was a lovely girl, and the man who had loved her was dead because of her impulsive action. Her terrible adventure had not only disgraced her physically, but may have given her moral wounds. The scars from these wounds may never have healed completely.

After these sad events, on God's command Jacob moved

---

his family away from the site of the crime to Bethel. There he once again became the man he ought to have been earlier, a father who led his family in the service of God.

Dinah's story occurred about 1,900 years before Christ's birth. But the dangers she encountered are not just restricted to that period of time or to the Book of Genesis. The problem Dinah faced is universal. Modern cities continue to allure young girls eager to "experience life." All too often, though, the experience of life for a young girl in a strange city turns into an encounter with the harsh realities of sin from which she—and her family—may never fully recover.

Nearly 2,000 years later, Paul warned Timothy that young widows who easily become bored begin to go from house to house, gossiping and committing other sins. Thus they begin to oppose God and further Satan's work (1 Timothy 5:13-15). Paul also gave Titus specific instructions for young women, in order to keep them from discrediting God's Word (Titus 2:4-5).

Dinah, a girl whose curiosity led to crime and mourning
(Genesis 34:1-15, 24-29)

Questions:
1. Compare Genesis 34:1-3 with Genesis 12:14-20; 20:1-18; 26:7-11. How do Sarah's and Rebekah's situations compare to Dinah's?
2. To which dangers did Dinah, a Hebrew girl, expose herself when she traveled to the city of Shechem?
3. Briefly but completely describe the consequences of Dinah's trip to herself and to others.
4. Why does God place such high demands on virginity? (Deuteronomy 22:13-24)
5. What do you consider to be the most important lesson in this story?
6. How can you apply a principle you have learned in this story to your daily life?

John Scanzoni

Tamar,
a neglected woman who vindicated
her rights

Genesis 38:6-30 Now Judah took a wife for Er his first-born,
and her name was Tamar. But Er, Judah's first-born, was evil
in the sight of the Lord, so the Lord took his life. Then Judah
said to Onan, "Go in to your brother's wife, and perform your
duty as a brother-in-law to her, and raise up offspring for
your brother." And Onan knew that the offspring would not
be his; so it came about that when he went in to his brother's
wife, he wasted his seed on the ground, in order not to give
offspring to his brother. But what he did was displeasing in
the sight of the Lord; so He took his life also.

Then Judah said to his daughter-in-law Tamar, "Remain a
widow in your father's house until my son Shelah grows up";
for he thought, "I am afraid that he too may die like his
brothers." So Tamar went and lived in her father's house.

Now after a considerable time Shua's daughter, the wife of
Judah, died; and when the time of mourning was ended,
Judah went up to his sheepshearers at Timnah, he and his
friend Hirah the Adullamite. And it was told to Tamar,
"Behold, your father-in-law is going up to Timnah to shear
his sheep."

*From "Assertiveness for Christian Women" by John Scanzoni, *Christianity To-
day*, June 4, 1976, page 17. Copyright 1976 by *Christianity Today*. Used by permission.

So she removed her widow's garments and covered herself with a veil, and wrapped herself, and sat in the gateway of Enaim, which is on the road to Timnah; for she saw that Shelah had grown up, and she had not been given to him as a wife. When Judah saw her, he thought she was a harlot, for she had covered her face.

So he turned aside to her by the road, and said, "Here now, let me come in to you"; for he did not know that she was his daughter-in-law. And she said, "What will you give me, that you may come in to me?" He said, therefore, "I will send you a kid from the flock." She said, moreover, "Will you give a pledge until you send it?" And he said, "What pledge shall I give you?" And she said, "Your seal and your cord, and your staff that is in your hand." So he gave them to her, and went in to her, and she conceived by him.

Then she arose and departed, and removed her veil and put on her widow's garments. When Judah sent the kid by his friend the Adullamite, to receive the pledge from the woman's hand, he did not find her. And he asked the men of her place, saying, "Where is the temple prostitute who was by the road at Enaim?" But they said, "There has been no temple prostitute here."

So he returned to Judah, and said, "I did not find her; and furthermore, the men of the place said, 'There has been no temple prostitute here.'" Then Judah said, "Let her keep them, lest we become a laughingstock. After all, I sent this kid, but you did not find her."

Now it was about three months later that Judah was informed, "Your daughter-in-law Tamar has played the harlot, and behold, she is also with child by harlotry." Then Judah said, "Bring her out and let her be burned!" It was while she was being brought out that she sent to her father-in-law, saying, "I am with child by the man to whom these things belong." And she said, "Please examine and see, whose signet ring and cords and staff are these?"

And Judah recognized them, and said, "She is more righteous than I, inasmuch as I did not give her to my son Shelah." And he did not have relations with her again. And it came about at the time she was giving birth, that behold, there were twins in her womb. Moreover, it took place while she was giving birth, one put out a hand, and the midwife took and tied a scarlet thread on his hand, saying, "This one came out first." But it came about as he drew back his hand, that behold, his brother came out. Then she said, "What a breach you have made for yourself!" So he was named Perez. And afterward his brother came out who had the scarlet thread on his hand; and he was named Zerah.

Tamar, whose name meant "palm tree," adjusted her long dress. Held together with a girdle tied around her waist, the folds flowed around her slim figure and nearly touched the ground. She glanced pensively at the widow's dress she had just taken off, and then remembered that her veil had to be put on just right.

Again Tamar looked at herself. Years ago she had often worn colorful clothing, but now she hardly remembered the joy of those occasions. Although she looked younger in this outfit, there was no joy in her glance. Her eyes were serious, and around her mouth were lines of unspoken grief. She was a lonely and neglected widow.

Her movements were resolute; she knew what she wanted. She had weighed the consequences of the decision that had slowly ripened within her and knew the costs could be high. With a heavy heart, she was about to carry out a plan that she had hoped to avoid entirely.

The time had come for her to seek her rights, out of necessity, because no one else was looking after her interests. For years she had been waiting for a word from her father-in-law, Judah, but the word never came. *Judah,* she mused, *would rather forget me entirely.* Therefore, she was on her way to meet him.

As Tamar closed the door of her parental home where she had been living, she relived some of the experiences she once had with Judah and his sons.

How proud she had been when Judah had chosen her to be the bride of Er, his eldest son. Judah was the son of Jacob, the honored elder who had come to live in Canaan from the far country of Mesopotamia. Next to his riches

The land of Mesopotamia was located in the country we now call Iraq. The name "Mesopotamia" is taken from the Hebrew words Aram-naharaim, which mean "Aram of the two rivers," for it was bordered by the Euphrates River on the west and the Tigris River on the east (Genesis 24:10, marginal note). and many sons, Jacob was known for his worship of the God of heaven and earth. He and his family did not serve sun- or moon-gods, nor idols of wood and stone. The eternal God was their Lord and that made them special.

Naturally, these factors had aroused Tamar's expectations. She had considered herself privileged to marry Er. But everything had gone differently than she had hoped. Her new husband did not prove to be a godly man at all. In fact, his deeds so aroused God's anger that He took Er's life.

The laws of the tribe to which Tamar now belonged prohibited a childless woman from remaining a widow. The leaders believed that the name of a man could not, under any circumstances, go into oblivion.

Being a daughter-in-law, Tamar remained under the authority of her father-in-law after the death of her husband. It was his job to arrange Tamar's second marriage, like the first. "Marry your sister-in-law, Tamar," he said to his second son, Onan. "Our law requires this of a dead man's brother; so that her sons from you will be your brother's heirs."[1]

Onan fulfilled his duty and married her, but in appearance only. Their marriage was in fact only a sham. By purposely preventing his new wife's pregnancy, Onan refused to keep the memory of his brother alive and to bring new heirs into the world.

Thus he caused Tamar great sorrow. He not only insulted her, but also injured God's institution of holy matrimony. He intentionally sabotaged the continuation of Judah's offspring. He did this not once, but over and over again.

God could not forgive this sin, especially since the promised Messiah would come out of the tribe of Judah. This prediction would be clearly foretold later, at the death of Jacob.[2] How much Judah and his sons were already aware of this fact is not known. But the unknown future did

1. Genesis 38:8
2. Genesis 49:8-10

not make Onan's attitude any less despicable.

After Onan, like his brother Er, had been put to death by God for his sins, Tamar became a widow for the second time. Her trust in religion and in men in general had been badly damaged. The only person she still seemd to trust was Judah, her father-in-law.

"Wait to marry again until my youngest son, Shelah, has grown up," Judah had said. "Then he will become your husband."[3]

So Tamar returned to her parental home to wait until Shelah was old enough to marry her. It was the only thing a widow of that time could do. She could not live an independent life or pursue further personal development. A single woman or widow simply had to do what she was told to do.

The days became weeks, the weeks months, and the months years without producing a change in Tamar's circumstances. Gradually it dawned on Tamar that Shelah would never come for her. Judah was afraid that his youngest son would also die after marrying her, and so would prevent his coming. Tamar began to understand that people blamed her for the deaths of her two husbands. Rather than recognizing the misbehavior of his sons, Judah was placing the blame on her.

With the dawn of recognition, Tamar stopped trusting Judah. Blocked out of the whole affair of her marriage, she had never been asked for an opinion. No one had even inquired about her feelings. She was only considered to be a woman without rights, free to be treated by a man as he pleased. The curse pronounced on Eve, that the man would rule over the woman, also rested on her.[4]

But Tamar was not going to put up with such an attitude. Although hurt by the humiliating treatment she had received, she did not try to seek comfort from another husband. She respected her father-in-law's request, in spite of the fact that she knew that Shelah would not marry her for any price. She knew that Judah probably wanted to forget that her name had been registered in his tribe.

Understanding that when she took matters into her own

3. Genesis 38:11
4. Genesis 3:16

hands all the responsibility would shift on her, Tamar refused to neglect her duty. The command to fill the earth had been the first responsibility given to the man and the woman equally.[5] Just because the man was not fulfilling his God-given obligation, she felt, was no excuse for her to forsake her duties as well. As a human being, she would have to give a personal account of her action to God. Regardless of her freedom to escape that obligation, Tamar refused to compromise.

The duty to give birth to an heir weighed heavily on her. She understood intuitively that the extinction of Judah's tribe had to be prevented at all costs and considered what she was about to do a religious duty. For these reasons, Tamar prepared herself for a meeting with her father-in-law.

Later, in a comparable manner, other women would vindicate the rights of their tribes and be proven right by God (Numbers 27:1-11; 36:5-10). These women and Tamar received a place in history, for without them history would have run an entirely different course. Through Tamar's individual contribution and personal sacrifice, God's plan for the world was carried out. Her obedience pointed to Jesus Christ, through whose obedience God's plans for the salvation of men were realized (Isaiah 53:10).

Meanwhile, Judah was on his way from Adullam to Timnah. He looked forward to the days ahead of him. Like his forefathers, Abraham, Isaac, and Jacob, he was a wealthy shepherd and was going to Timnah to oversee the annual shepherding events. After the extensive work of shearing the sheep had been skillfully completed, there would be a great feast. For weeks everybody had been talking about this feast, for it would have an abundance of special food and drinks.

Judah became excited as he thought about the events to come. The time just behind him had not been without cares. For years, there was great sorrow in his life because of his dead sons. Recently the loss of his wife had added one more burden to his shoulders.

But the time of mourning was now past, and Judah wanted to relax. He wanted to take his place in society once more. So he traveled in full array. His identification seal which hung around his neck on a silver and gold cord

5. Genesis 1:28

showed passersby that he was a distinguished man. In his hand was the staff, a token of dignity showing that he was the head of his tribe.

As he walked, he noticed a woman on the side of the road near the entrance to the village of Enaim. A veil covered her face and prevented any meeting from having a personal touch. *She is a prostitute,* thought Judah. The woman's veil didn't bother him, for he was not interested in contacting the woman as a person. She only aroused his desires for an object to satisfy his sexual needs.

With the promised reward of a young goat in return for her sexual services, the woman agreed to the act. It was the usual payment offered for this sin, and Judah expected that it would be sacrificed in the temple of the goddess of fertility, to whom prostitutes often dedicated themselves.

The woman, however, was not prepared to believe him at his word. Apparently she feared that the promised goat would fail to arrive. "What pledge will you give me, so that I can be sure that you will send it?" she asked.[6] Judah left the choice with her. When she requested the signs of his honor and dignity—his identification seal and his walking stick—he handed them to her without hesitation!

After they had met, Judah continued on his way toward Timnah. Tamar—for it was indeed she—returned to her parental home and exchanged her veil for her widow's clothing. Life continued as if nothing had happened, at least for a while.

When Judah, by means of a friend, delivered the goat in exchange for the seal and the staff, he was unable to find the woman. When he asked the men of Enaim during his investigation where he could find the prostitute, they were astonished. "A prostitute?" they answered. "No, we do not know her. We have never had one here!"

Judah, who had not allowed God to guide his actions in this situation, now feared what other people would say. If they found out what he had done, he would certainly become a laughingstock among his people. With impact it dawned on him how he had been blinded by his sexual

6. Genesis 38:17

desires. He had acted thoughtlessly and had put his reputation at stake. The only thing left for him to do was to forget the situation entirely, hoping there would be no further consequences to him. He tried to forget that the woman, also, could suffer consequences for her moral transgression. He knew that she could lose her life for her sin. Later that punishment would be laid down in God's laws.

Three months later the storm broke over Tamar's head. By then, her father-in-law had heard that she was pregnant, clearly as a result of immorality. Judah's fury knew no bounds, and he was right. Tamar had stained the name of his tribe. She was the widow of his two eldest sons and was still considered to be the future bride of his youngest son. As the head of the family, he held the responsibility to judge the sin Tamar had committed. No one can disregard the holy institution of marriage without being punished.[7]

His judgment was ruthless, inexorable. Tamar had to suffer the strongest punishment that could be applied to her transgression. Without inquiring after the facts of her case, Judah sentenced her to death. "Bring her out and burn her," he shouted.[8]

Was this judgment tainted by a mingling of fear and anger? Did Judah take into account his own thoughts toward Tamar in connection with the death of his sons? Would the burning of Tamar also burn his feelings of self-accusation, the result of his breach of promise concerning Shelah and her?

Calm and dignified, Tamar appeared in her widow's dress. Shortly before she arrived at the site of execution, she gave something to one of the men escorting her. "Take these things to my father-in-law," she said, and handed him an identification seal and a staff. "Ask him if he recognizes them," she continued with emphasis. "Tell him that the man who owns these is the father of my child."[9]

Judah's reaction was revealing. He was appalled. His own sin was crudely exposed by his personal effects. He couldn't conceal it any longer. He had to confess with shame that Tamar had vindicated the legal rights that he

7. Hebrews 13:4
8. Genesis 38:24
9. Genesis 38:25

had kept from her. "She is more in the right than I am," he acknowledged, "because I refused to keep my promise to give her to my son Shelah."[10]

Did Judah remember that he was the one who was truly guilty? She had not seduced him; he had taken her. His deed was motivated by unlawful physical desire, while her motives had been noble. She had been thinking of the continuation of Israel's posterity. From her viewpoint, she had simply done what she had thought to be her duty.

If Judah had been more honest with himself, he would have had to acknowledge that he had used two measuring sticks. He had used a double standard and wanted to see Tamar killed for an offense he had also committed himself.

Judah's sin of hypocrisy is something with which all humans have to wrestle. The Apostle Paul strongly condemns those who judge others for the same sins they themselves commit (Romans 2:1-2).

Six months later, Tamar brought two sons into the world, Perez and Zerah. A marriage with Shelah was now out of the question, as well as being redundant. Judah had served as his replacement. Shelah did not have to marry Tamar, for justice had been done.

Many years later, Matthew wrote down the genealogy of Jesus Christ.[11] It is a long list of names, mainly of men. Of the five women mentioned, Tamar is the first. Mary, the mother of Jesus, closes the list.

Tamar, the abused woman, is the first registered woman in the genealogy of Jesus Christ. Her son Perez became a forefather in the lineage of Jesus of Nazareth. This fact is not proof that God approved of sin. But it does confirm the fact that He wrote His history straight through the failings of men.

The Bible is not a gallery of heroes. It gives the accounts of sinful people who experienced, much to their happy surprise, that they could fit into the plan God had for this world. God's plans found their beginning and completion, their fulfillment, in Jesus Christ.

Christ's love for human beings was also proven by the publication of this genealogy. As far as His earthly life was

10. Genesis 38:26
11. Matthew 1:1-17

concerned, Christ not only was prepared to come from a family of men and women of dubious quality, but was also willing to emphasize that point in order to demonstrate the depth of His love. He was not afraid to identify with every sinful person who played a part in His earthly background.

Christ also did something very special for women in general while He was on earth. He gave them back their position, their value. He gave them back the place God had originally made for them before Eve's fall in the garden. He approached them with respect, without prejudice, and treated every woman with objectivity and love. He nailed unequal treatment between men and women to the cross. Double moral standards were foreign and offensive to Him.

One day, for example, the Jewish leaders brought a woman to Him who had been caught in the very act of adultery.[12] Behind their pious pretext to obey the law of Moses which says that a woman should be killed for such an offense, they were trying to trap Jesus and condemn the woman at the same time.

Jesus did not excuse the sin the woman had committed. He did, however, expose her accusers. "All right," he said sternly. "Hurl the stones at her until she dies. But only he who has never sinned may throw the first!"[13]

The accusers of the woman did not begin to heave rocks. Instead, they moved stealthily away. The Saviour had touched them in their very hearts by revealing their dishonest and unloving prejudice.

Tamar's story only gains perspective when the light of Jesus Christ shines on it. In spite of everything that can be said against her, Tamar became an enviable woman. Jesus Christ extended to her the honor of becoming a mother in the early history of His earthly family.

12. John 8:3-10
13. John 8:7

Tamar, a neglected woman who vindicated her rights
(Genesis 38:6-30)

Questions:
1. Study the story of the daughters of Zelophehad (Numbers 27:1-11; 36). What was the reason for their request and what was the result? What relation do you see between this situation and Tamar's?
2. Do you see any relation between what is said of Christ in Isaiah 53:10 and Tamar? If so, what?
3. Study the story of Judah and Tamar in light of Romans 2:1-2. What is your conclusion?
4. Which five women do you encounter in the lineage of Jesus in Matthew 1:1-17? Write out what you know about them.
5. What light does the inclusion of these women in the genealogy throw on the person of Christ?
6. In this story you have examined many biblical principles. What was the most important one for you? How are you going to apply it to your own life?

7

*"When all kinds of trials and temptations crowd into your lives, my brothers, don't resent them as intruders, but welcome them as friends! Realize that they come to test your faith."**

James

Jochebed, a woman who learned to consider sorrow a friend

Exodus 1:8-22 Now a new king arose over Egypt, who did not know Joseph. And he said to his people, "Behold, the people of the sons of Israel are more and mightier than we. Come, let us deal wisely with them, lest they multiply and in the event of war, they also join themselves to those who hate us, and fight against us, and depart from the land."

So they appointed taskmasters over them to afflict them with hard labor. And they built for Pharaoh storage cities, Pithom and Raamses. But the more they afflicted them, the more they multiplied and the more they spread out, so that they were in dread of the sons of Israel. And the Egyptians compelled the sons of Israel to labor vigorously; and they made their lives bitter with hard labor in mortar and bricks and at all kinds of labor in the field, all their labors which they rigorously imposed on them.

Then the king of Egypt spoke to the Hebrew midwives, one of whom was named Shiphrah, and the other was named Puah; and he said, "When you are helping the Hebrew women to give birth and see them upon the birthstool, if it is

*James 1:2-3. J. B. Phillips, *The New Testament in Modern English, Revised Edition,* Copyright © J. B. Phillips 1958, 1960, 1972. Published by Macmillan Publishing Company, New York, and Collins Publishers, London. Used by permission.

a son, then you shall put him to death; but if it is a daughter, then she shall live." But the midwives feared God, and did not do as the king of Egypt had commanded them, but let the boys live. So the king of Egypt called for the midwives, and said to them, "Why have you done this thing, and let the boys live?" And the midwives said to Pharaoh, "Because the Hebrew women are not as the Egyptian women; for they are vigorous, and they give birth before the midwife can get to them."

So God was good to the midwives, and the people multiplied, and became very mighty. And it came about because the midwives feared God, that He established households for them. Then Pharaoh commanded all his people, saying, "Every son who is born you are to cast into the Nile, and every daughter you are to keep alive."

Exodus 2:1-10 Now a man from the house of Levi went and married a daughter of Levi. And the woman conceived and bore a son; and when she saw that he was beautiful, she hid him for three months. But when she could hide him no longer, she got him a wicker basket and covered it over with tar and pitch. Then she put the child into it, and set it among the reeds by the bank of the Nile. And his sister stood at a distance to find out what would happen to him.

Then the daughter of Pharaoh came down to bathe at the Nile, with her maidens walking alongside the Nile; and she saw the basket among the reeds and sent her maid, and she brought it to her. When she opened it, she saw the child, and behold, the boy was crying. And she had pity on him and said, "This is one of the Hebrews' children." Then his sister said to Pharaoh's daughter, "Shall I go and call a nurse for you from the Hebrew women, that she may nurse the child for you?"

And Pharaoh's daughter said to her, "Go ahead." So the girl went and called the child's mother. Then Pharaoh's daughter said to her, "Take this child away and nurse him for me and I shall give you your wages." So the woman took the child and nursed him. And the child grew, and she brought him to Pharaoh's daughter, and he became her son. And she named him Moses, and said, "Because I drew him out of the water."

The cry of a newborn baby cut through the home.

Mother Jochebed[1] sunk into her pillows, tired. At the same time a feeling of new motherly happiness flowed through her. She had once again brought a child into the world. Jehovah! His Name be praised! This was the moment she had been waiting for with great expectation, for which she had hoped and also feared. "Is it a boy or a girl?" she asked anxiously.

Before the answer came, Jochebed was distracted by sounds from outside. A whip cracked through the air and unmercifully cut the back of one of her fellow citizens. She heard a Hebrew screaming and the loud cursing of a furious Egyptian. Such sounds had become more familiar, and their penetration into the houses of the Hebrew colony resulted in fear and tension. The situation of the Israelites in the Egyptian province of Goshen had not been rosy for a long time and recently had become increasingly worse.

At first the Egyptians had favored the Hebrews, largely due to the influence of Joseph, the son of Jacob. Through his insight and wise leadership, Egypt had withstood an immense famine and at that time the Egyptians had felt greatly obliged to him. Their country became a haven of refuge for the entire Near East.[2] Years after Joseph died, the Egyptians continued to appreciate the Israelites.

Four centuries had passed since then, and the situation had gradually changed. But God continued to bless His people in the foreign land. Israel's numbers increased and her property holdings became larger and larger. As a result of this blessing resting on Israel, the Egyptians began to feel threatened. They tightened their control over the Hebrews, and tried to limit the Israelites' growth by suppression and forced hard labor. But their attempts continually failed. The Israelites began to multiply even faster than before.

Finally Pharaoh tried to approach the problem at its roots. To assist him, he called for the help of the two Hebrew midwives who helped the Israelite mothers with their deliveries. "Watch carefully whether a boy or a girl is born," he order, anger rising in his voice. "If it is a boy you

---

1. Numbers 26:59
2. Genesis 41:55-57

must kill him, but let the girls live."[3]

That cruel order also failed to produce results, for the midwives showed more fear toward God than for their king. They waved aside his orders with an excuse. "The Hebrew women have their babies so quickly that we cannot get there in time," they said. "They are not slow like the Egyptian women."[4]

The situation had not changed three years later when the first son of Amram and Jochebed was born. Since the midwives refused to cooperate, the king now gave a new order, this time to the entire nation. "From now on," he decreed, "throw all Hebrew boys that are born in the Nile."[5]

The order appalled the already pressured Israelites. For the Hebrew women, it changed the joy of new motherhood into a dreadful tension. From that point on, their baby boys' first cries of life were directly followed by their death screams when their warm, little bodies were drowned in the chilly waters of the Nile. With horror the parents had to watch, over and over again, their newly born children eaten by crocodiles.

"Crocodile food," shuddered Jochebed. "That is what Pharaoh makes of our flesh and blood." Then with a shock she came back to the reality of her own situation. Although only a few seconds had passed since her question, she sensed that the midwife was hesitant to answer. When the woman looked at her, Jochebed discovered fear in her eyes. "It is a boy," she finally said with a sigh, compassion ringing through her voice.

"Give me the child," was all Jochebed could utter. A moment later she pressed the soft, pink little body to her heart. "What a beautiful child you are," she whispered. Then, as she looked her baby over from head to toe, a strange awareness came over her. This was not simply a beautiful baby; this sound child was in a special way related to God's plans. He was beautiful for God.[6]

God did have plans for her little son. Jochebed could not define precisely what those plans would be, but she knew it

3. Exodus 1:16   5. Exodus 1:22
4. Exodus 1:19   6. Acts 7:20

for sure. From that moment on she decided to fight for his life. The overtone within her heart would not be sorrow. She would trust in God.

Jochebed and her husband were Levites and thus belonged to the tribe which would later be assigned to serve God in His temple. Although both of them were born into slavery, they had kept their faith in God. Jochebed continually directed the antenna of her faith toward Him. Because of this faithfulness, she received His messages and gained inner convictions about things which would be revealed later.

God was about to do something great for the world, for the suppressed Hebrews, and for this tested family. And, as He usually does in history, He drew a human being into His plan, Jochebed. Much would depend on her faith, in the degree to which she was attuned to His leading.

The Bible shows that God honored Jochebed and her husband. Their faith gave them the courage to ignore the king's command.[7] They obeyed a higher leadership, God. Against Pharaoh's expressed order, they hid their child day after day after day. Their motivation was obedience to God, as well as love for the child.

What is faith? It is the confident assurance that something we hope for will happen. It is the certainty that what we hope for is waiting for us even though the possibility seems slim (Hebrews 11:1). All Christians have been justified by faith through Christ (Galatians 2:16), but in order to receive answers to their prayers, they must pray with faith (Matthew 21:21). If they doubt and do not pray with faith, however, their prayers will go unanswered because whatever is done apart from faith is sin (Romans 14:23).

What did they expect? A miracle? That solution no doubt lay within the possibilities. God, who created man and animals as well as the entire creation out of nothing, had the power to do anything. His power was not shortened. Every possibility was available to Him.

Gradually Jochebed began to understand that God was going to work a miracle through her. Yet for the time being everything remained the same. The atmosphere in the country continued to be oppressive and hostile against the Hebrews. The king had not become indulgent. Every day it

7. Hebrews 11:23

became more difficult to hide the baby from the outside world. His tiny voice became stronger and his daily periods of crying increasingly became a matter of concern.

Jochebed could not possibly imagine how fascinating God's orders were for this child uniquely called by Him. "Every child comes into the world with 'sealed orders.' Every human being has a unique destiny to fulfill."* That she daily bathed, clothed, and fed a child who would become one of the world's greatest national leaders was still sealed. God had chosen her son to become one of the greatest personalities of the Old Testament. As a man, he would pass on God's laws to the Hebrew people, laws that centuries later would still be considered the foundation of society. He foreshadowed God's Son—the Messiah to come—and the first development of the realization of these facts had been placed in the hands of his mother.

Although the problems of God's people at this time in history seemed insurmountable, they were nearing their end. God had plans, but no problems. His plans would be announced through this child.

During the days which came and went, insecurity and faith fought for precedence. There were human insecurities concerning the child, and there was the assurance of faith. This testing period made Jochebed's faith grow and gave her courage.

Her growing faith made her inventive. She became skilled in hiding the child and in developing ideas to spare his life. She learned how to educate little Aaron so that he wouldn't betray his baby brother. She managed to get along well with Miriam, her only daughter, despite all the details of taking care of the baby. God also had sealed orders for her other children, whose futures were closely connected with that of the baby's. Jochebed was responsible for their development as well as for that of her baby son.

The plan that Jochebed developed was simple and close at hand. Based on facts which she had carefully put together, the plan was above all inspired by faith. God Himself had prompted ideas in her mind which made the plan genial and,

*Reprinted by permission from *The Christian Family* by Larry Christenson, page 64, published and copyright 1970, Bethany Fellowship, Inc., Minneapolis, Minnesota 55438.

as it turned out, slightly humorous.

First she transformed a simple box of reed—maybe her shopping basket—into a little boat. The outside of papyrus reeds had to protect the baby against crocodiles that seemed to have little interest in eating reeds. Then she carefully coated the inside of the box with waterproof bitumen and tar. The water that was threatening the tiny boy with death must save his life. It must become the baby's ally and friend.

Calmly and carefully, Jochebed went to work. Every possibility was thought through. Gradually, as she developed her own good solutions, she fell in step with the plans God had formed in heaven for His servant on earth. Her part in His plan was vitally important, but she could only move in the directions He pointed out to her.

Because of Jochebed's faith, problems didn't have a chance to develop. They didn't paralyze or isolate her. On the contrary, her trials paved the way to greater possibilities. Her difficulties became her friends instead of her enemies.

Jochebed made the salvation of her youngest child a family affair. Through her approach, the problems and concerns became a blessing to the entire family. Her husband was one with her in her faith. Yet it was she, the mother, who especially put her seal on the members of the family during this difficult time and welded them together as instruments for God.

She had the courage to involve her young daughter in her plans. That also was a step of faith. When she placed the little boat in the waters of the Nile River, Jochebed took her hands off her son and placed him into the care of God. The future of her little boy now lay solely in His hands and those of little Miriam.

Miriam unobtrusively kept watch over the floating cradle, demonstrating how carefully she had been trained for this task. The poise and trust of the mother characterized the daughter.

When Pharaoh's daughter noticed the box and had it

picked up out of the Nile, Miriam conducted herself in an exceptionally mature manner. As soon as she saw that her brother was safe with the princess, she stepped forward. No word or motion betrayed how personally she was related to this child. The sound of her voice was controlled. Her behavior created no suspicion. "Shall I go and find one of the Hebrew women to nurse the baby for you?" she asked.[8]

"Yes," the princess answered,[9] having no idea that with those words she gave the child back to its mother. After the child had grown older and the princess had adopted him as her own son, she named him Moses. "That will be his name," she said, "because I have drawn him out of the water."[10]

So during a time of terrible persecution, Jochebed was able to care for her son openly without feeling threatened. She was even being paid for her care by the daughter of the man who had tried to kill her child. That was divine humor.

Moses had been rescued; his future was completely secure. After the early years under his mother's care, he received the best opportunities at Pharaoh's court that any young man of his time could have wished for. He, the son of a slave Hebrew family, received the education of a prince. All the possibilities of the mighty and learned Egyptians were at his disposal. And, while Hebrew babies were still dying premature deaths, Moses was being prepared for the task for which God had chosen him. His sealed order was to become the redeemer of his people.

Jochebed continued to have a part in that preparation. The few years that Moses had been under her wings helped to determine his future. Her faith in God had become familiar to him. The patriarchal traditions of his people and their complete commitment to God made an indelible impression on his receptive soul; the attractions of the heathen palace had little to offer him.

When Moses became a grown man, he preferred the sufferings of his people above the riches of Egypt. He developed into a man of faith[11] who walked daily with the unseen God as if he could see Him. He became a "friend of

8. Exodus 2:7   10. Exodus 2:10
9. Exodus 2:8   11. Hebrews 11:24-29

God."[12] This was an exceptional compliment to be given to a human being.

Jochebed had received the meaning of her name, "Jehovah is her glory." Had that name been given to her by believing parents in the hope that she would work for God's glory in her life? Did she choose it herself as a public witness of her deepest thoughts, or was it a name of honor granted to her by God?

The Bible mentions her name only twice,[13] but it is forever engraved in history as the name of one of the most important mothers who ever lived. Probably never in history have three children of one mother, Jochebed, ever had such an influence at the same time.

Her children demonstrated to the world the place that God had in their mother's heart. His honor had been her highest purpose. They also illustrated that principle with their own lives. When Moses was the leader of the Israelite nation,[14] Aaron was its high priest who symbolized God's holiness and grace toward His people.[15] As the high priest, he also represented God to the people and the people to God. As the intercessor for his people, he also foreshadowed Christ.[16]

Miriam also played a part in the leadership of God's people, which for a woman was a rare exception in Israel's history. She was the nation's first prophetess, and used her gifts in music and song to allow the Hebrew women to bring honor to God.[17]

So Jochebed's three children used their lives in the service of God. Their mother had the laws of God in her heart long before they could be read from a printed page and imprinted them in the hearts of her children as the Bible commands.[18] She accomplished her feats and ministries by believing the promises of God.

Jochebed lived far too early to be familiar with the words of James: "When all kinds of trials and temptations crowd into your lives, my brothers, don't resent them as intruders, but welcome them as friends! Realize that they come to test your faith."[19] But she did experience the truth of his words,

12. Exodus 33:11
13. Exodus 6:20; Numbers 26:59
14. Micah 6:4; Psalm 106:23
15. Exodus 28:1
16. Hebrews 2:17; 5:1-5
17. Exodus 15:20-21
18. Deuteronomy 6:6-7
19. James 1:2-3

just like the other men and women—heroes of faith—in whose ranks she is listed. They were common people who became famous because of their faith. They were capable of unusual and great achievements because they believed in the almighty God.[20]

Despite often hostile environments, they thought vertically instead of horizontally, spiritually instead of according to their own human natures. Convinced that their God was greater than the greatest difficulty, they courageously faced immense problems. They experienced how much God desired to surprise them, and what a small thing it was for Him to change their threatening enemies into friends.

Jochebed, a woman who learned to consider sorrow a friend (Exodus 1:8-22; 2:1-10)

Questions:
1. Why is the mother of Moses listed in the ranks of the heroes of faith? (Hebrews 11:23)
2. What is faith, according to Hebrews 11:1? In what ways do you see this faith realized in Jochebed's life?
3. Consider Jochebed's life in light of Genesis 50:20 and Romans 8:28. Explain how these verses came true in Jochebed's life.
4. Think through her situation carefully and list all the "enemies" Jochebed faced.
5. Write down which of these "enemies" turned into "friends."
6. Do you have certain difficult circumstances in your life that God's power and grace could change into "friends"? If so, what are they?

20. Hebrews 11:1-40

"Usually the man is responsible for leadership. Here it is a woman. God does not always work according to a set pattern. He is looking for people who are available as His instruments."
The Author

Deborah, a leader of a nation who was inspired by faith

Judges 4:1-10 Then the sons of Israel again did evil in the sight of the Lord, after Ehud died. And the Lord sold them into the hand of Jabin, king of Canaan, who reigned in Hazor; and the commander of his army was Sisera, who lived in Harosheth-hagoyim. And the sons of Israel cried to the Lord; for he had nine hundred iron chariots, and he oppressed the sons of Israel severely for twenty years.

Now Deborah, a prophetess, the wife of Lappidoth, was judging Israel at that time. And she used to sit under the palm tree of Deborah between Ramah and Bethel in the hill country of Ephraim; and the sons of Israel came up to her for judgment. Now she sent and summoned Barak the son of Abinoam from Kedesh-naphtali, and said to him, "Behold, the Lord, the God of Israel, has commanded, 'Go and march to Mount Tabor, and take with you ten thousand men from the sons of Naphtali and from the sons of Zebulun. And I will draw out to you Sisera, the commander of Jabin's army, with his chariots and his many troops to the river Kishon; and I will give him into your hand.' " Then Barak said to her, "If you will go with me, then I will go; but if you will not go with me, I will not go." And she said, "I will surely go with you; nevertheless, the honor shall not be yours on the journey that you are about to take, for the Lord will sell Sisera into the hands of a woman." Then Deborah arose and went with Barak to Kedesh. And Barak called Zebulun and Naphtali together to Kedesh, and ten thousand men went up with him; Deborah also went up with him.

Judges 4:12-16 Then they told Sisera that Barak the son of Abinoam had gone up to Mount Tabor. And Sisera called together all his chariots, nine hundred iron chariots, and all the people who were with him, from Harosheth-hagoyim to the river Kishon. And Deborah said to Barak, "Arise! For this is the day in which the Lord has given Sisera into your hands; behold, the Lord has gone out before you." So Barak went down from Mount Tabor with ten thousand men following him. And the Lord routed Sisera and all his chariots and all his army, with the edge of the sword before Barak; and Sisera alighted from his chariot and fled away on foot. But Barak pursued the chariots and the army as far as Harosheth-hagoyim, and all the army of Sisera fell by the edge of the sword; not even one was left.

Judges 4:23-24 So God subdued on that day Jabin the king of Canaan before the sons of Israel. And the hand of the sons of Israel pressed heavier and heavier upon Jabin the king of Canaan, until they had destroyed Jabin the king of Canaan.

(Also read the remaining verses of Judges 4—5.)

The situation in Israel was gloomy and desolate. Life had become nearly unbearable and unsettled. All trade was paralyzed as caravans stopped traveling through the valley of Jezreel to the south or east. Farming was limited to the minimum. Hardly a farmer dared to till his ground for fear of being killed during a surprise enemy attack.

With traffic at a standstill, the streets were deserted. The inhabitants of the mountain villages moved outside their homes a little more often than the others, but they still preferred to use the narrow side paths.

For more than 20 years the land had been occupied and the conquerors had kept the people firmly under their thumbs. Young people knew the word "freedom" only from the mouths of their parents. For the older people, it was getting increasingly difficult to remember what that word really meant. The population was downhearted, fearful, and depressed.

King Jabin, who lived in the northern city of Hazor, dominated all of Israel. His dreaded right-hand man, General Sisera, commanded a large army which had 900 chariots.[1] Everyone was afraid of him, for his forces could overrun and trample down the countryside swiftly and with deadly intent. Only the mountain people were relatively safe, for his chariots could not reach them.

The cause of this misery, however, did not lie with the occupation forces but with the Israelite people themselves. After 80 years of prosperity under the previous rulers, Judges Ehud and Shamgar, the Israelites had shown no gratitude toward God. They fell away from Him and started to worship idols.

The results of their actions were predictable. The people who thought that they no longer needed God now had to experience His distance.[2] When He withdrew His protection, they became powerless against their enemies and peace disappeared.

Yet not all of the roads in the country were deserted. One was walked on quite frequently. In the hill country of Ephraim, on the road between Bethel and Ramah, more and more people were going to a palm tree which stood plainly above the surrounding shrubbery. Under that tree, their present leader—the prophetess Deborah—held court, judged the people, and gave direction to their lives.[3] She was the only woman judge among the 12 judges who ruled between the times of Joshua and Samuel.

She held a two-fold position among her people. She was both their national and spiritual leader and carried out her duties capably and with good results. Like so many times before in their tumultuous history, distress in their lives was

1. Judges 4:3
2. Judges 4:2
3. Judges 4:4-5

causing the Israelites to seek God. In this situation, Deborah had the privilege of being His instrument. Because of her faith, the events that happened changed history.

Deborah's responsibilities were those of a man. She hadn't arrived at her position by subduing a man, however, and had not appropriated power illegally. Her responsibilities had been given to her by God. She had been appointed to bring the people back to God, to liberate them from the power of their oppressors. The entire nation acknowledged her as its leader. Therefore, as Deborah judged in spiritual and material affairs, she also instructed her people in the things of God.

She was the wife of Lappidoth, who assumed a minor role. In the events which were to follow, she would be the principal leader. Among the people of her time—men and women alike—she was as exceptional as the palm tree in her land which was later named after her. She was outstanding and unique.

Prophetess Deborah was the mediator between God and His people, the proclaimer of His Word. In her high position, she communicated insight, wisdom, and the knowledge of God with love to her people. With the fine-tuned intuition of a person who abides in the presence of God, she sensed that God's time had come to throw off the yoke of oppression.

"A wise man's heart discerns both time and judgment," wrote Solomon.[4] Deborah proved that statement correct. She not only discerned the time of God's action in the history of her people, but also received insight into the very method He wanted to use to liberate them.

She felt, and rightly so, that as a woman she was not the appointed person to fight this war. So the command went out to Barak, the son of Abinoam of Kedesh, "Mobilize 10,000 men."[5]

Deborah thought and made her decisions based on her walk with God. Her leadership had form and content. She performed her tasks brilliantly, intelligently, and with self-sacrificial perseverance.

4. Ecclesiastes 8:5
5. Judges 4:6

For years as God's messenger she worked toward freedom and prayed for it. But now that the time had come for it to be realized, someone else was to play the lead role. With wisdom and tact, Deborah found the right way to approach Barak.

She understood that all human authority was, in fact, delegated authority. The only one who had real and final authority was God. So, although she was first among her people, Deborah did not place herself over Barak. Instead she placed herself next to him and together with him placed herself under God's leadership. As she walked with God, she lost the desire to share all the glory. Other people became more important to her. She executed leadership by inspiring others.

She derived her motivation from the God of Israel. Never, not even for a single moment, did she doubt that the Almighty One—who had rescued His people out of their problems in the past—would help them again.

Her command to Barak was at the same time an encouragement. "Don't be afraid because of their number," she said confidently. "Looking at it from God's point of view, our enemy is defeated already. The chariots and the forces of Jabin are nothing in the sight of God. The only thing He expects from you is faith."[6] In a couple of sentences, she placed the situation in its proper perspective.

Deborah's tactful, spiritual leadership had a freeing effect on Barak. It kept him from showing himself to be stronger than he was. He dared to accept the challenge, but not without Deborah. He was certain that God would be fighting for his forces only if she accompanied him. He acknowledged her as his superior in faith and courage. Yet, because of these experiences, he developed into a man who is named among the heroes of faith in Hebrews 11.[7] He became a strong leader in the coming war.

Although Deborah's approach helped Barak become a hero for God, neither of them allowed thoughts of rancor or competition to come between them. They functioned in God's plan as instruments. Together as two people—a

6. Judges 4:6-7
7. Hebrews 11:32-33

woman and a man[8]—they carried out God's orders. Each gave in voluntarily to the other for the well-being of the entire nation. They also knew that part of God's plan included their deliverance through a woman, Jael, the wife of Heber.[9]

Deborah and Barak functioned as one unit. Mutually they helped and completed each other. Together they moved from Ephraim to Kedesh, which was not far from where Jabin lived. There Barak recruited his soldiers. At the head of the newly formed army, Barak and Deborah climbed up the side of Mount Tabor together and looked down across the plains of Jezreel to their enemy camped at the foot of the mountain.

Throughout her constant cooperation with Barak, Deborah had remained the leader and the person responsible for all decisions. When the day to fight had come, God revealed His will through her. "Rise up," she said to Barak, "for this is the day that the Lord has given Sisera into your hands."[10] Again she followed up her command with encouragement. "Has not the Lord gone out before you? Don't be afraid of Sisera. This is not a fight between you and him but between him and God. The outcome of the battle is decided before it has begun. The victory is God's. He fights on your side."[11]

Deborah then watched as Barak, with his 10,000-man force behind him, stormed down the steep flank of Mount Tabor. Next to the Kishon River, he met Sisera's army arrayed behind the grim and armored chariots. The enemy expected an easy victory. Wasn't their opponent laughably small, an unworthy foe?

Had anyone looked toward the sky while the two armies were coming together? Gray thunderclouds moved together, rumbling ominously. Bad weather was at hand.

The storm broke in all its ferocity precisely at the moment the Israelites reached the plain. Heavy rain and hailstones beat into the faces of the enemy soldiers.* Before long the Kishon River overflowed its banks and became a

---

*Flavius Josephus, *Antiquities of the Jews,* Book V, Chapter 5.

8. Genesis 1:26-28   10. Judges 4:14
9. Judges 4:9   11. Judges 4:14

wide stream. Wildly moving water churned the ground under the warriors' feet into a muddy mess. The chariots of the enemy stuck fast, bringing defeat instead of victory. The routed enemy was unable to make a quick escape because of the pileup of chariots.

Barak and his men acknowledged God's hand in what was happening. They pursued the enemy with even more determination and killed every last man.[12] Sisera, seeing that all was lost, saw a chance to escape and ran for cover. But even he did not escape. He fell, like Deborah had predicted, by the hand of Jael.[13]

The occupation was over. Israel was free again. The oppression was gone. Normal living could finally take its course. Life had color and meaning again. The people had new goals; their future looked bright.

It is a known fact that it is hard for any man to stand up under adversity. Yet the character of a man is possibly even more tested when he is asked to execute power.

Since creation, God has decreed that a woman and a man —united through marriage—should carry out His commission on earth. She was created as a partner with man, equal to him and yet different. Therefore she is suitable for him, capable of completing him.

This partnership between man and woman can reach complete fulfillment within marriage. But it can also take place in other places. Society has always functioned best when man and woman carried out their God-given tasks harmoniously. Deborah and Barak demonstrated that principle.

Usually the man has been responsible for leadership. But in this passage, a woman was the leader. God does not always work according to a set pattern. He is looking for people who are willing to be used as instruments in any way He chooses.

Deborah didn't unduly execute her power. She simply lived up to her responsibilities. She was a fascinating and gifted woman who executed her varied tasks capably. A woman of enormous spiritual strength, she instructed her

12. Judges 4:16
13. Judges 4:18-21

people in the laws of God. But she also turned around and gave skillful guidelines for a military operation. She knew how to use the sword as well as the pen.

Deborah's greatest strengths, however, were not her human capabilities, no matter how striking and many-sided they were. She knew that her strength and power were delegated to her by God. In everything she did, her expectation came from Him. Such people, written about in Isaiah,[14] continue to draw new strength over and over again despite their many exertions.

Deborah's victory song, which belongs to some of the oldest and most beautiful of Hebrew poetry, proved that her strength was in God. Her happiness was not, first and foremost, based on the deserved satisfaction of a task well-done. Her deepest joy came from God.

"Listen, O you kings and princes, for I shall sing about the Lord, the God of Israel," the song of Deborah and Barak began.[15] It ended with these words: "But may those who love the Lord shine as the sun when he goes forth in his might."[16]

Deborah's life was strong and sparkling. Describing such a life, Solomon wrote, "The path of the just is as the shining light that shines more and more unto the perfect day."[17]

Although God had first place in Deborah's epic song, she left a lot of room for her fellowmen. Everyone who had a part in the victory—Barak, the leaders of the people, Jael—were elaborately mentioned.

Deborah did not claim honor for herself. Soberly she ascertained the fact that there were no leaders in Israel till she had arrived. How did she describe herself? She simply considered herself to be a mother in Israel. Just as a mother's attentions are directed toward the well-being of her children, the deep desires of Deborah's heart were directed toward the welfare of her people.

Deborah is one of the outstanding women in biblical history because of her leadership, her character, and her beautiful poetry. Certainly she had a fascinating life. But her priorities were not based on her accomplishments. The

---

14. Isaiah 40:31
15. Judges 5:1-3
16. Judges 5:31
17. Proverbs 4:18

open secret of her life was God. More than anything else, she showed what a woman can do when God is in complete control of her life. The possibilities are many-sided for a leader of a nation who wants to be inspired through faith in God.

Deborah, a leader of a nation who was inspired by faith (Judges 4:1-10, 12-16, 23-24)

Questions:
1. Study Deborah's life carefully. What are her positive characteristics?
2. Do you also see negative characteristics? If so, what are they?
3. What does Deborah's victory song tell about her views of God? (Judges 5)
4. How much emphasis does she place in her song on other people? How much on herself?
5. Write down what you can find concerning her cooperation with Barak. What impresses you most about their relationship?
6. List any practical principles you learned from this story. How are you going to apply them?

9

*"And I discovered more bitter than death the woman
whose heart is snares and nets, whose hands are chains.
One who is pleasing to God will escape from her,
but the sinner will be captured by her."**
Solomon

Delilah,
a woman who deliberately ruined
a spiritual leader

Judges 16:4-30 After this it came about that he loved a woman in the valley of Sorek, whose name was Delilah. And the lords of the Philistines came up to her, and said to her, "Entice him, and see where his great strength lies and how we may overpower him that we may bind him to afflict him. Then we will each give you eleven hundred pieces of silver." So Delilah said to Samson, "Please tell me where your great strength is and how you may be bound to afflict you." And Samson said to her, "If they bind me with seven fresh cords that have not been dried, then I shall become weak and be like any other man."

Then the lords of the Philistines brought up to her seven fresh cords that had not been dried, and she bound him with them. Now she had men lying in wait in an inner room. And she said to him, "The Philistines are upon you, Samson!" But he snapped the cords as a string of tow snaps when it touches fire. So his strength was not discovered. Then Delilah said to Samson, "Behold, you have deceived me and told me lies; now please tell me, how you may be bound." And he said to her, "If they bind me tightly with new ropes

*Ecclesiastes 7:26.

which have not been used, then I shall become weak and be like any other man."

So Delilah took new ropes and bound him with them and said to him, "The Philistines are upon you, Samson!" For the men were lying in wait in the inner room. But he snapped the ropes from his arms like a thread. Then Delilah said to Samson, "Up to now you have deceived me and told me lies; tell me how you may be bound." And he said to her, "If you weave the seven locks of my hair with the web and fasten it with a pin, then I shall become weak and be like any other man." So while he slept, Delilah took the seven locks of his hair and wove them into the web. And she fastened it with the pin, and said to him, "The Philistines are upon you, Samson!" But he awoke from his sleep and pulled out the pin of the loom and the web.

Then she said to him, "How can you say, 'I love you,' when your heart is not with me? You have deceived me these three times and have not told me where your great strength is." And it came about when she pressed him daily with her words and urged him, that his soul was annoyed to death. So he told her all that was in his heart and said to her, "A razor has never come on my head, for I have been a Nazirite to God from my mother's womb. If I am shaved, then my strength will leave me and I shall become weak and be like any other man."

When Delilah saw that he had told her all that was in his heart, she sent and called the lords of the Philistines, saying, "Come up once more, for he has told me all that is in his heart." Then the lords of the Philistines came up to her, and brought the money in their hands. And she made him sleep on her knees, and called for a man and had him shave off the seven locks of his hair. Then she began to afflict him, and his strength left him. And she said, "The Philistines are upon you, Samson!" And he awoke from his sleep and said, "I will go out as at other times and shake myself free." But he did not know that the Lord had departed from him.

Then the Philistines seized him and gouged out his eyes; and they brought him down to Gaza and bound him with bronze chains, and he was a grinder in the prison. However, the hair of his head began to grow again after it was shaved off. Now the lords of the Philistines assembled to offer a great sacrifice to Dagon their god, and to rejoice, for they said, "Our god has given Samson our enemy into our hands." When the people saw him, they praised their god, for they said, "Our god has given our enemy into our hands, even the destroyer of our country, who has slain many of us."

It so happened when they were in high spirits, that they said, "Call for Samson, that he may amuse us." So they called for Samson from the prison, and he entertained them. And they made him stand between the pillars. Then Samson said to the boy who was holding his hand, "Let me feel the pillars on which the house rests, that I may lean against them." Now the house was full of men and women, and all the lords of the Philistines were there. And about 3,000 men and women were on the roof looking on while Samson was amusing them. Then Samson called to the Lord and said, "O Lord God, please remember me and please strengthen me just this time, O God, that I may at once be avenged of the Philistines for my two eyes." And Samson grasped the two middle pillars on which the house rested, and braced himself against them, the one with his right hand and the other with his left. And Samson said, "Let me die with the Philistines!" And he bent with all his might so that the house fell on the lords and all the people who were in it. So the dead whom he killed at his death were more than those whom he killed in his life.

Delilah was a Philistine woman who belonged to a culture that worshiped idols. She was also a woman who didn't take morality seriously. Having little respect for her body, she threw away her honor casually like a prostitute.

The Bible doesn't mention these facts as clearly as it does about Rahab,[1] but the context does allow these conclusions.

Delilah is remembered as a woman who ruined a spiritual leader. As a woman, she had been created by God to be a companion for man, his co-worker. But she deliberately degraded herself to be his opposition, to cause his misfortune. What motivated her to damage Samson, the man in her life, so irreparably?

Samson was an extraordinary man, a servant of God. He

1. Joshua 2:1

was called a Nazirite, a man dedicated to God even before his birth.[2] His long hair demonstrated this commitment and for 20 years he ruled and judged over his Israelite people.[3]

Samson's name, which meant "little sun," showed how happy his parents had been when he was born. His birth, like that of Jesus many centuries later,[4] was announced by an angel. It was also the result of a miracle, since his mother initially could not have children. After his birth, Samson developed under the blessing of God into a leader—the mightiest man of Judah—and possessed unusual physical strength.[5] Thus he was far ahead of his enemies, who rightly considered him to be unconquerable. Hadn't God said that Samson would begin to deliver Israel from the hand of the Philistines?

In spite of his physical strength, Samson was morally weak. The man who easily ripped a lion apart with his bare hands had no control over his sexual passions. Samson had loosened the necessary brake on his behavior toward the opposite sex, a move that is dangerous for a man and sometimes fatal for a spiritual leader.

Different women before Delilah had already exerted a bad influence on his life. Now he fell into her hands and became involved. He didn't marry her. He didn't take her as his wife into his own house. Instead he became her lover and lived with her.

The leaders of the Philistines, probably one for each of their large cities, heard about Samson's relations with Delilah. So they drew Delilah into a conspiracy to produce his downfall. After all, it had become a national necessity for them to kill Samson. Where military force had failed, slyness now had to succeed.

The leaders visited Delilah personally and said, "Try to find out what makes Samson so strong. Talk with him till you know. Then we can overpower him and subdue him."[6]

Was it Delilah's love of money that made her accept the proposal? Each of the men promised her 1,100 pieces of silver. Since every piece weighed over 16 grams, the total weight of silver promised would be an inconceivable sum.

2. Judges 13:2-5, 24-25
3. Judges 16:31
4. Luke 1:26-38
5. Judges 14:5-6; 15:13-16
6. Judges 16:5

Or were Delilah's actions caused by bitterness against the Israelites? Samson's future as a leader of a nation that had always proven itself stronger than her people because of God's help now lay in her hands. The God of Israel was not her God, for she and her people worshiped the idol Dagon.

The love of money is a real danger. Moses stated that a person who accepts a bribe becomes blinded (Exodus 23:8), and Paul called the love of money "a root of all sorts of evil" (1 Timothy 6:10). Those who seek money for its own sake become pierced with many sorrows.

The request of the Philistine leaders also must have appealed to her pride. In a country and period of history where a woman's position lagged far behind a man's, the important leaders of her country were knocking on her door for help.

After she accepted their proposal, Delilah went about finding the secret of Samson's strength. She began her deceit with every means that she as a woman had at her disposal. Her first step was flattery. "Please tell me what makes you so strong," she begged. "Is there anyone who could ever capture you?"[7]

Blinded by his feelings for Delilah, Samson unwisely answered her. He clearly underestimated the danger he was in. If he had been in close contact with God, he would have become alarmed and quickly left her.

Through Delilah's insolence, the leaders of her people witnessed her humiliating game with Samson from an adjoining room. They listened intently as she bound him with seven raw-leather bowstrings. But when she called out, "The Philistines are upon you, Samson," he snapped the bowstrings like cotton thread.[8] The leaders, realizing that the plan had failed, remained where they were.

Delilah then worked on Samson's honesty. "You are making fun of me," she sulked. "You told me a lie."[9] Samson once again listened to her and played her dangerous game. But once again the ropes with which she had tied him broke like spiderwebs when he used his muscles.

Living with a man who proved that he cared about her did not change Delilah's thoughts. It did not soften her character. On the contrary, everything she had—her allure-

7. Judges 16:6
8. Judges 16:9
9. Judges 16:10

ment, her brains—were willfully and unchangingly directed toward Samson's destruction.

Again she continued her attempts to trap Samson, this time by weaving his hair into her loom. Once again she had no results. Although the Philistine leaders had become impatient and returned to their cities, Delilah had enough patience left to try one more plan of attack.

Now she played the role of a woman whose feelings of love had been hurt. "You say that you love me," she whined, "but you don't confide in me. You have betrayed me these three times now and you still haven't told me what makes you so strong."[10]

She based her new attack on her passionate lover's reaction when his love was doubted. As a woman, she had a weapon against which few men could stand. This she now put into effect. Daily she sulked, nagging at him without interruption. Constantly she accused him about his tricks.

She knew how to use this final weapon with conviction and with success. Gradually she broke Samson's resistance. He became like wax in her arms. Finally, utterly frustrated, he could not stand it any longer. He could think of only one thing, *I want to stop this sulking. I want peace!*[11]

Then he told her the whole truth. "My power is connected with my long hair. It has never been cut," he confessed. "Since before my birth I have been dedicated to God. My strength lies in my commitment to Him. My hair is a symbol of that. Cut off my hair and I am no different from any other man."[12]

Sensing that this time Samson was speaking the truth and was not holding anything back, she relentlessly sent a message to the Philistine leaders. "You must come once more," she said. "This time he has told me everything."[13] At no time did she have second thoughts about betraying her lover.

The men came quickly with their money. Once again they hid themselves. Again Delilah did what Samson had told her to do. She called in someone to cut off his seven locks of hair while he was sleeping on her knees. Even while the hair

---

10. Judges 16:15   12. Judges 16:17
11. Judges 16:16   13. Judges 16:18

was being cut, Delilah felt that she had won. When his hair dropped to the ground, Samson's strength left him.

When Delilah screamed out, "Samson, the Philistines are here to capture you,"[14] for a moment Samson didn't realize his defeat. Like the other times, he tried to shake himself free. But this time his struggles were in vain. After his hair was cut, the Lord left him.[15] He lost his tremendous strength—and the presence of God—through his own mistakes.

The results were appalling. The Philistines captured Samson. They didn't kill him but they gouged out his eyes. From then on he went on through life mutilated; empty sockets saw nothing but darkness.

As a token of their triumph and Samson's shame, the leaders sent him to the city of Gaza. As if the humiliation of his blindness and imprisonment were not enough, he was put to work grinding grain like a common slave.

Delilah had done her work thoroughly. Samson, a servant of God and a ruler in Israel, was tarnished. Hardly a deeper degradation for this giant could have been imagined.

His people shared his suffering. After Samson's rule ended, they entered a period of defeat, anarchy, and spiritual decline. His tarnish became theirs.

Samson had denied his God, his ideals, and his people. He had become a betrayer of himself and the cause for which he stood. Naturally he only had himself to blame for his deeds. But that did not make Delilah any less guilty. Like every other person, Delilah was personally responsible before God for her deeds. She remained accountable for her share in the disaster that struck Samson and others.

The only fact that could be mentioned in Delilah's defense is that she didn't know God. She didn't have His laws. Yet, even as a heathen woman, she had little excuse.

Through Paul, God says that the heathen who don't possess His laws nevertheless have them written in their hearts and will be judged accordingly (Romans 2:13-15).

Solomon, nearly two centuries later, characterized the relationship between Delilah and Samson. "And I found

14. Judges 16:20
15. Judges 16:20

more bitter than death the woman whose heart is snares and nets, whose hands are chains. One who is pleasing to God will escape her, but the sinner will be captured by her."[16]

Delilah's portrait resembles the bad woman Solomon warns about in Proverbs. "For the lips of an adulteress drip honey," he writes, "and smoother than oil is her speech. But in the end she is bitter as wormwood . . . . Her feet go down to death."[17]

Delilah's feet did indeed lead to death, literally. The death which was awaiting Samson and thousands of other people would soon be disclosed in the future.

The city leaders were out of themselves for joy. To celebrate their capture of Samson, they declared a great festival and dedicated it to their god Dagon. Once the festival had begun, the people became excited and called for Samson. They wanted to make fun of and humiliate him. They wanted to exalt Dagon over the God of Israel. When Samson finally arrived, didn't anyone notice that his hair had been growing? Was there no one who had carefully watched a man so definitely their superior?

The large festival building was completely filled with men and women and, of course, the Philistine leaders. Probably even Delilah was there, for how could they celebrate such an enormous feast without the heroine? Just the flat roof of the building held about 3,000 people.

Was there no one in the crowd who remembered the God of Israel and of Samson? Was there no fear that He would avenge the insult paid to Him, His servant, and His people?

When the Philistines forced Samson to stand between the two pillars supporting the roof so that they could mock him, Samson remembered his former calling. Wasn't he appointed to redeem his people from their enemies? "O Lord, Jehovah," he prayed, "remember me again. Please strengthen me one more time so that I may pay back the Philistines for the loss of my eyes."[18] At the same time he pushed against the pillars with all his might and they crumbled. The entire building which had been supported by them crashed down, killing Samson and thousands of

16. Ecclesiastes 7:26
17. Proverbs 5:3-4
18. Judges 16:28

Philistines.

The catastrophe Delilah had brought about and through which she probably lost her life undoubtedly reached much further than she had anticipated or desired. What had begun with immorality, as in the story of Dinah,[19] ended with the deaths of many people. The outcome of her deeds was worse than the beginning.

"A harlot is a deep pit,"[20] Solomon wrote. "None who go to her return again, nor do they reach the paths of life."[21] Fellowship with a prostitute is like carrying a fire in one's chest.[22] Can anyone do that without being burned?

In her book *The Unique World of Women*, author Eugenia Price writes that the Christian women of today possibly feel themselves far removed from the treacherous and vile Delilah. They are, she believes, convinced that they have nothing in common with Delilah. Eugenia then warns women not to make a serious mistake. "We may not be harlots, or even overtly conniving and deceitful as Delilah was, but many of us *are* deceitful . . . . In fact, I think all of us have streaks of deception."*

Centuries after Samson's and Delilah's deaths, Paul gave another warning to the Christians in Corinth which also applies to our perspective concerning Delilah's life. "From this lesson we are warned that we must not desire evil things as they did."[23] It is wise not to ignore these warnings.

*From *The Unique World of Women* by Eugenia Price, page 63. Copyright © 1969 by Zondervan Publishing House. Used by permission.

19. Genesis 34:1-30
20. Proverbs 23:27   22. Proverbs 6:27
21. Proverbs 2:19   23. 1 Corinthians 10:6

Delilah, a woman who deliberately ruined a spiritual leader
(Judges 16:4-30)

Questions:

1. Consider Delilah's life in light of Proverbs 5:1-11. Which of the negative things mentioned there apply to her?
2. Do you see good or bad characteristics in Delilah which are not mentioned in Proverbs 5:1-11? If so, list them.
3. Write down all the results of Delilah's deeds. Which one stands out?
4. Now describe Delilah's life as you see it.
5. What valuable lessons or warnings can you draw from her life?
6. How can you apply in your life what you have learned?

10

"Let no one ever come to you without coming away better and happier. Be the living expression of God's kindness: kindness in your face, kindness in your eyes, kindness in your smile, kindness in your warm greeting."*

Mother Teresa

Naomi,
a widow who cared about the well-being
of others

Ruth 1:1-6 Now it came about in the days when the judges governed, that there was a famine in the land. And a certain man of Bethlehem in Judah went to sojourn in the land of Moab with his wife and his two sons. And the name of the man was Elimelech, and the name of his wife, Naomi; and the names of his two sons were Mahlon and Chilion, Ephrathites of Bethlehem in Judah.

Now they entered the land of Moab and remained there. Then Elimelech, Naomi's husband, died; and she was left with her two sons. And they took for themselves Moabite women as wives; the name of the one was Orpah and the name of the other Ruth. And they lived there about ten years. Then both Mahlon and Chilion also died; and the woman was bereft of her two children and her husband. Then she arose with her daughters-in-law that she might return from the land of Moab, for she had heard in the land of Moab that the Lord had visited His people in giving them food.

Ruth 1:15-22 Then she [Naomi] said, "Behold, your sister-in-law has gone back to her people and her gods; return after

*Malcolm Muggeridge, *Something Beautiful For God,* page 69. Copyright © 1971 by The Mother Teresa Committee, Harper & Row, Publishers, Inc., New York. Used by permission.

your sister-in-law." But Ruth said, "Do not urge me to leave you or turn back from following you; for where you go, I will go, and where you lodge, I will lodge. Your people shall be my people, and your God, my God. Where you die, I will die, and there I will be buried. Thus may the Lord do to me, and worse, if anything but death parts you and me."

When she [Naomi] saw that she [Ruth] was determined to go with her, she said no more to her. So they both went until they came to Bethlehem. And it came about when they had come to Bethlehem, that all the city was stirred because of them, and the women said, "Is this Naomi?" And she said to them, "Do not call me Naomi; call me Mara, for the Almighty has dealt very bitterly with me. I went out full, but the Lord has brought me back empty. Why do you call me Naomi, since the Lord has witnessed against me and the Almighty has afflicted me?" So Naomi returned, and with her Ruth the Moabitess, her daughter-in-law, who returned from the land of Moab. And they came to Bethlehem at the beginning of barley harvest.

Ruth 4:14-17 Then the women said to Naomi, "Blessed is the Lord who has not left you without a redeemer today, and may his name become famous in Israel. May he also be to you a restorer of life and a sustainer of your old age; for your daughter-in-law, who loves you and is better to you than seven sons, has given birth to him." Then Naomi took the child and laid him in her lap, and became his nurse. And the neighbor women gave him a name, saying, "A son has been born to Naomi!" So they named him Obed. He is the father of Jesse, the father of David.

(Also read the entire Book of Ruth.)

Naomi, the widow of Elimelech, looked affectionately at the newborn baby on her lap. Usually not at a loss for words, she now found none to express her gratitude. Her emotions were overflowing.

Around her buzzed the voices of excited neighbor women. "Ruth has a son," they shouted happily. "Praise the Lord, Naomi. In your old age there will be a man to take care of you. But far more important, there is a redeemer for your family. We pray," continued the women, "that this little boy will become famous in Israel."[1]

Naomi laughed. The name of her husband, which meant "my God is king," would continue to be passed on. His inheritance would not be given to others. The names of her dead sons would not be forgotten.

She looked again at the little baby. He had been named Obed, which meant "servant." She prayed silently that the Lord God of Israel would truly be king in Obed's life. Then she thought of Elimelech and a flood of memories pressed themselves on her.

Reflecting back, she saw herself traveling with her husband and two sons from Judah to Moab many years earlier to escape the famine that had broken out in Israel. This famine was so widespread that even in their city of Bethlehem (called "the house of bread"), there had hardly been any food available, in spite of the fact that the city was considered to be the granary of the country.

Elimelech had felt the responsibility for his family heavily, especially since his sons, Mahlon and Chilion, were both sick and slowly wasting away. "Let's emigrate," Elimelech had proposed. "Let's go to Moab, where there will be food for all of us. There we won't have to worry."[2]

How differently everything had turned out, Naomi thought.

Moab was the country east of the Dead Sea inhabited by the descendants of Lot, the nephew of the Patriarch Abraham.[3] It was not just a neighboring country. It was a nation which God had cursed because its people had been cruel toward the Israelites after their exodus from Egypt.[4] A Moabite was unholy in the sight of God and as such was not allowed to enter the assembly of the Lord.

Among these people, Elimelech, Naomi, and their sons made their home. But after they had been there only a short time, Elimelech died.

Since they were living in Moab, the sons took wives from among the Moabites. Mahlon married Ruth and Chilion married Orpah. As the years passed, though, Naomi

---

1. Ruth 4:14   3. Genesis 19:36-37
2. Ruth 1:1   4. Deuteronomy 23:3-4; Jeremiah 48:1-47

became painfully aware that both marriages had remained childless. *Is God keeping His blessing from us?* she asked herself. Like every Israelite, she believed that children were a blessing from God and that the withholding of them was a proof of His curse.[5]

Then Chilion and Mahlon, her only children, died while still young men. Within a period of 10 years, all this sorrow had come on her. Naturally she had been lonely. Alone—away from her country, deprived of her family, forsaken by God—she had anticipated a bleak future without meaning or perspective.

Then she had heard that food was once again plentiful in Bethlehem. God was blessing His people by giving them good crops. This miracle had confirmed her suspicions. The famine in the past had indeed been God's warning to His disobedient people.[6]

She had realized that her family's departure from Bethlehem had, in fact, been a journey away from God. In Bethlehem she and Elimelech had been prominent citizens. *If only we had confessed our sins before God,* she thought, *perhaps we could have led our people back to Him.* But her family had missed their chance by leaving the country.

In light of God's laws, the marriage of her sons had not been acceptable. An Israelite who married a foreigner acted against the commandments of God,[7] who had given this instruction to keep His people from wandering away from Him.

Naomi's conviction had continued to grow stronger. *I must go back,* she thought. *I can no longer stay in this foreign country. I belong in Israel, in Bethlehem.*

Although she had suffered from the deaths of her family, she had also experienced rich blessings in the persons of Orpha and Ruth. When Naomi prepared herself to return to her homeland, both young women had, without hesitation, decided to leave their parents and go with her.

Naomi had always felt a strong responsibility for those women because they were the widows of her deceased sons. But that had not been the only reason. They were also

5. Deuteronomy 28:4, 18
6. Leviticus 26:14-20
7. Deuteronomy 7:3-4

heathen women who did not know God. She had often shared with them her faith in God, the God whom she had grieved but still loved intensely in spite of everything.

The interest in Orpah and Ruth had also helped her forget her own sorrow. It had been good to be mindful of the well-being of others; she had become refreshed from her giving. Shortly thereafter they had left Moab.

On the way to Bethlehem, Naomi had suddenly become aware of the finality of her daughters-in-law's decisions. Weren't their futures totally dependent on new marriages for each of them?

Certainly the thought that her daughters-in-law might one day belong to other husbands had been painful. The always dormant suffering from the deaths of her sons had surfaced once again. But simultaneously her thoughts about the well-being of Ruth and Orpah had overruled. Gradually, as the thoughts about her sons had moved to the background, she wanted their widows to find opportunities for new happiness.

Yet Orpah and Ruth, knowing the facts, had chosen to go with her. Instead of returning to their homes where they would find happiness, they sought to enter a country prejudiced against them. No law-abiding Israelite would even consider the possibility of marrying a Moabitess.

"Go back to your homes, to your parents," Naomi had begged. "May the Lord reward you for your faithfulness to your husbands and to me."[8]

Orpah and Ruth, however, had totally rejected her proposal. "No," they had answered tearfully. "We want to go with you to your people."[9]

Naomi, however, had not changed her mind, not even after her own future flashed before her. Her life would be even emptier. Not only would she be without a husband and children; she would also lose her daughters-in-law. But God had given her the grace not to be selfish and so she was willing to sacrifice her desires for a secure life in old age for the welfare of the two women.

The three widows had stood together on a lonely, sun-

8. Ruth 1:8-13
9. Ruth 1:10

bathed road, each unable to master her tearful emotions. Suddenly one of the standing figures had moved. Orpah had walked up to Naomi, embraced her, and then turned back toward Moab. Ruth had then approached her mother-in-law and clung to her.

"Please go back like your sister-in-law," Naomi had said.[10] But Ruth had vehemently shaken her head.

"Don't urge me to leave you, for I want to go wherever you go, and live wherever you live. Your people shall be my people, and your God shall be my God," Ruth had said.[11]

"Your God shall be my God." These words had deeply touched Naomi. They proved that Ruth had not only chosen to stay with her mother-in-law, but she had also chosen the God of Israel. Naomi's words about God had been heard and understood. Despite Naomi's backsliding, God had blessed her words. That itself was marvelous grace, an unmerited favor.

In spite of this encouraging experience, her arrival in Bethlehem had been a disappointment. The news of her return had traveled quickly. It stirred the entire city. "Have you heard the news?" the people had shouted to one another. "Naomi is back!"[12] In spite of her long absence abroad, the people still remembered her. Was she not related to Boaz, their rich fellow-citizen?

The reactions of the people when they first greeted her had shown Naomi how much she had changed. "Is this Naomi?" the women had asked in disbelief.[13] Through their eyes, she had seen herself mirrored. She had become a woman with an inanimate face on which sorrow had etched deep furrows. Her personality had lost all color. Her name meant "pleasant," but clearly her joy had gone and the people of Bethlehem knew it.

"Do not call me Naomi; call me Mara," she had answered impulsively.[14] The name Mara meant "bitter" and that was the way she had felt at that moment. That was the name she wanted to be called. But her bitterness stemmed from self-pity, and self-pity usually blames someone else. This is also what had happened to Naomi. Her pent-up feel-

10. Ruth 1:15
11. Ruth 1:16
12. Ruth 1:19
13. Ruth 1:19
14. Ruth 1:20

ings of sorrow and despair had given way to an accusation against God. "The Almighty has dealt very bitterly with me," she said. "I went out full, but the Lord has brought me back empty."[15]

She didn't say a word about the fact that Elimelech and she had moved away from God when they had traveled to Moab. At that moment, she had not yet realized that she had not returned empty. She now had a loving daughter-in-law who wanted to share her life.

From that moment on, however, her life had begun to change. As obviously as God's blessing had been absent in Moab, it became evident in Bethlehem.

She had often mused about the words that Moses, the Law-giver, had been given by God to say. "I am giving you the choice today," he had said, "between God's blessing or God's curse! There will be a blessing if you obey the commandments of the Lord your God which I am giving you today, and a curse if you refuse them and worship the gods of these other nations."[16]

Naomi had experienced God's blessing through Ruth, who from the beginning had cared for her like a daughter. She had also seen God's blessing through His leading. From the first moment, He had led them both toward Boaz, the man who would radically change their lives.

When Naomi became aware of God's dealings with them and suspected that He was giving Ruth the joy of a new marriage with Boaz, she had said to Ruth, "My dear, isn't it time that I try to find a husband for you, and get you happily married again?"[17]

Boaz was a rich landlord but, even more important, he was a man who feared the Lord. Once he fell in love with Ruth, he had shown no hesitancy to marry her. As a result of the marriage, little Obed now sat on her lap. Ruth, whose marriage with Mahlon had remained childless, now had been blessed by God with a child.

The child's movement stopped Naomi's musing about the past. The neighbor women had all said. "A son has been born to Ruth."[18] She smiled at the "grandson" who did not

15. Ruth 1:20-21   17. Ruth 3:1
16. Deuteronomy 11:26-28   18. Ruth 4:15

even have the slightest trace of her blood in his veins. This thought did not make her bitter. She didn't poison her pleasure with thoughts of what could have been. She didn't say that she would have been happier holding Mahlon and Ruth's child.

Naomi accepted the facts. She opened her heart to Obed as if he were her own grandson. After all, he was the son of Ruth, who was more precious to her than seven sons. That in itself was complete happiness and so she was grateful. According to Jewish law, on the other hand, she did have a grandson, for Obed was counted as the son of Mahlon.

Naomi's future was finally bright. Every thought about loneliness disappeared like snow before the sun. Ruth, for whom she had lovingly cared, now did everything she could to bring her mother-in-law happiness. The grandmother was taking care of the child instead of the mother.

Naomi once more became the pleasant one again, a person who gave and received love. The Mara period now lay behind her. "Blessed is the Lord," the neighbor women had said, [19] and these words stayed in her heart. God had been good to her in spite of hardships, sorrows, and her own failures.

How good had He been? She had no idea at this time that the sprawling child on her lap would become a special link in the history of her people and in the history of redemption. How could she even imagine that she was cherishing the grandfather of Israel's most beloved king, David? Only the future would reveal that with David the birth of the Messiah would come into sight. Naomi, who was mindful of the well-being of others, did not have the faintest idea that her life would be connected with the Saviour of the world, Jesus Christ, who would come over a thousand years after her.

19. Ruth 4:14

Naomi, a widow who cared about the well-being of others
(Ruth 1:1-6, 15-22; 4:14-17; also read the entire Book of
Ruth.)

Questions:
1. Write out a brief biography of Naomi's life.
2. What are the positive aspects of her life? What are
   some negative ones?
3. Why was Naomi a good mother-in-law?
4. When you examine the statements Naomi made about
   God, what conclusions can you draw?
5. What do you believe influenced her life the most?
6. Which characteristics of Naomi would you like to
   develop in your own life? How will you do it?

11

*"Our lives will go on for millions and millions of years. And the choice we make now decides the type of life we are going to live in the future."**
Billy Graham

Orpah, who sank into oblivion because of a wrong decision

Ruth 1:1-15 Now it came about in the days when the judges governed, that there was a famine in the land. And a certain man of Bethlehem in Judah went to sojourn in the land of Moab with his wife and his two sons. And the name of the man was Elimelech, and the name of his wife, Naomi; and the names of his two sons were Mahlon and Chilion, Ephrathites of Bethlehem in Judah. Now they entered the land of Moab and remained there.

Then Elimelech, Naomi's husband, died; and she was left with her two sons. And they took for themselves Moabite women as wives; the name of the one was Orpah and the name of the other Ruth. And they lived there about ten years. Then both Mahlon and Chilion also died; and the woman was bereft of her two children and her husband.

Then she arose with her daughters-in-law that she might return from the land of Moab, for she had heard in the land of Moab that the Lord had visited His people in giving them food. So she departed from the place where she was, and her two daughters-in-law with her; and they went on the way to return to the land of Judah. And Naomi said to her two

*Billy Graham, *The Challenge,* pages 71-72. Copyright 1969 by Doubleday & Company, Inc., Garden City, New York, and World's Work Ltd., England. Used by permission.

daughters-in-law, "Go, return each of you to her mother's house. May the Lord deal kindly with you as you have dealt with the dead and with me. May the Lord grant that you may find rest, each in the house of her husband." Then she kissed them, and they lifted up their voices and wept. And they said to her, "No, but we will surely return with you to your people." But Naomi sàid, "Return, my daughters. Why should you go with me? Have I yet sons in my womb, that they may be your husbands? Return, my daughters! Go, for I am too old to have a husband. If I said I have hope, if I should even have a husband tonight and also bear sons, would you therefore wait until they were grown? Would you therefore refrain from marrying? No, my daughters; for it is harder for me than for you, for the hand of the Lord has gone forth against me." And they lifted up their voices and wept again; and Orpah kissed her mother-in-law, but Ruth clung to her. Then she said, "Behold, your sister-in-law has gone back to her people and her gods; return after your sister-in-law."

(Also read the entire Book of Ruth.)

Life had dealt harshly with Orpah. As a young woman she had already experienced a larger portion of suffering than many people do in a lifetime.

The death of her husband, Chilion, was the hardest blow to strike her. She had been a good wife for him, but their happiness had only lasted a few years. Since their marriage had been childless, after his death she was alone.

Within the circle of relatives, Orpha wasn't the only person who had experienced suffering. Naomi, her mother-in-law, was also a widow. Ruth, her sister-in-law, had shared the same experience. These three deaths had snatched away all the male members of the family. As a result a close tie had developed among these three bereaved women.

Orpah and Ruth were continually impressed with the love and unselfish attitude of their mother-in-law. Naomi, who among them had lost the most, gave herself fully to their well-being instead of looking to her own interests. Every day she proved that a good relationship between a mother-in-law and her daughters-in-law could exist.

But from now on Orpah would miss Naomi's loving care and the friendship and understanding of Ruth. The blessings that accompanied and softened her sorrow were now to be only memories, for Orpah had chosen to go back to her own people and to their gods.

We meet Orpah on a deserted country road somewhere in Moab, not far from the border of Israel. She was a lonely figure. When she looked back, she saw Naomi and Ruth moving away from her in the opposite direction. Then the horizon had swallowed up the diminishing dots they represented. They were gone, forever separated from Orpah.

Only a short time before, the three widows had walked together in the direction of the Israelite border. Now Orpah shuffled back down the road toward her homeland, alone.

Naomi's decision to return to Bethlehem hadn't come as a surprise for Orpah. *Was my mother-in-law ever really happy in Moab?* Orpah wondered. *In spite of her adjustment to the foreign country, Naomi always seemed to be uprooted and dispersed.*

Orpah knew this because of Naomi's relationship with God. Naomi was a Hebrew and did not worship the idols that the nations surrounding Israel did. She worshiped the true God who had chosen the Israelites to be His own people[1] and who had specifically given them the land in which they lived.[2] It was clear to Orpah that Naomi would only be happy in her own country, the land where her God was worshiped.

Both Ruth and Orpah had shared Naomi's decision to leave Moab and had left with her without hesitation. The three of them, originally united in their love for Mahlon and Chilion, belonged together.

So they began their journey. While their feet moved forward on the hot and dusty road, each of them entertained lingering thoughts of the past. Orpah's thoughts were with Chilion, the man she had loved. She missed him, especially now that her future was so uncertain.

1. Deuteronomy 7:6
2. Deuteronomy 1:8

Then, suddenly, Naomi stopped on the road. "Why don't you go back to the home of your parents?" she asked. "That is better, Orpah and Ruth, than coming with me. May God bless you for all the love you have shown my sons. May He reward you with another happy marriage."[3] To show her daughters-in-law that they had to take her words seriously, Naomi then kissed them good-bye. At that point all three of them burst into tears.

Ruth and Orpah didn't want to listen to Naomi's proposal. But Naomi's arguments were strong and logical. "Why should you come along with me? Your future lies within marriage. If you go with me, you will miss that opportunity. I am too old to have children," Naomi pleaded. "And, even if that were possible, because of their ages my sons would not be suitors for you."[4]

As they listened to this clear argument, both Orpah and Ruth began to cry again. But decisions became finalized. Ruth firmly decided to remain with Naomi, while Orpah, scared of the unknown future, was willing to be persuaded. After kissing her mother-in-law for the last time, Orpah turned around and began her journey back home. This is the last time that the Bible mentions her name.[5]

The Bible does not mention Orpah's reasons for her decision. It is clear, though, that till her separation she had not distinguished herself from Ruth in any way. Both of them are praised for their love toward their husbands. Both proved willing to leave their parental homes and their homeland to face an unknown future. Yet the circumstances had changed when a personal decision was suddenly demanded of them.

Why had Naomi, then, talked so urgently? Why did she paint the bare facts for Orpah and Ruth so clearly? Perhaps she knew that they would only be able to live happily in Israel if they had the chance to choose their new country voluntarily.

Through her own experiences, Naomi had learned that more than just a place to live or a person was at stake. Their choices were choices for or against God, and as such had to

.. Ruth 1:8-9
4. Ruth 1:11-13
5. Ruth 1:14

remain individual decisions based on personal conviction.

Joshua, a leader of the Hebrew nation, had emphasized that point before. "Decide today whom you will obey," he had declared. "Will it be the gods of your ancestors beyond the Euphrates or . . . ?" He then added, "But for me and my family, we will serve the Lord."[6]

Like Ruth, Orpah had come in contact with the God of Israel through the Hebrews. Unlike Ruth, however, she had decided not to serve God and was content to allow Him only to remain the religion of her husband and her in-laws. She did not want to accept Naomi's God as her God.

At the moment of decision, Orpah decided in favor of the god of her country, Chemosh, who was called "the abomination of Moab."[7] She preferred this god above the God of Israel. She chose a god who could not speak or act instead of the Creator of heaven and earth.[8] She turned her back on God—who wanted to show her His goodness—to serve vain idols.[9] She exchanged the God who gives life for an idol who claimed lives through child-sacrifices.

"Orpah has returned to her people and her gods."[10] With these words of Naomi, Orpah sank into oblivion. Her name disappeared from biblical writings.

The Bible clearly teaches that every decision a person makes has eternal consequences. These consequences not only influence his earthly life, but determine his eternal destiny. They decide whether he will go to heaven or to hell.

God keeps a record of everyone who has ever lived. In His Book of Life, He writes down every deed that they have done.[11] Any person whose name doesn't appear in that book will be committed to hell for eternity.

Perhaps Orpah later repented of her wrong decision and turned from her idols to God. If she sought to find Him with her whole heart, then doubtless He found her.[12] If, however, she did not seek God, then her future was over and she lost her life and her soul for eternity.

6. Joshua 24:15
7. 1 Kings 11:7
8. Isaiah 16:12
9. Jonah 2:8
10. Ruth 1:15
11. Malachi 3:16; Revelation 20:12-15
12. Jeremiah 29:13

Orpah, who sank into oblivion because of a wrong decision
(Ruth 1:1-15; also read the entire Book of Ruth.)

Questions:
1. What similarities of circumstances and attitudes do you see between Orpah and Ruth?
2. What is the remarkable difference between the two?
3. What words of Ruth express that difference most clearly?
4. Briefly explain the influence Ruth and Orpah had in history.
5. Study Orpah's life in light of Malachi 3:16-18 and Revelation 20:12-15 and write down your conclusions.
6. What did you learn from Orpah about making decisions? List a specific situation in which her example could influence a decision you will have to make.

12

"Every woman has the special privilege to be a 'power-station' for God to be used in any human dilemma. More than anything, people need loving. They thirst for LOVE."*
Brother Mandus

Ruth,
a woman characterized by loyalty

Ruth 2:1-23 Now Naomi had a kinsman of her husband, a man of great wealth, of the family of Elimelech, whose name was Boaz. And Ruth the Moabitess said to Naomi, "Please let me go to the field and glean among the ears of grain after one in whose sight I may find favor." And she said to her, "Go, my daughter." So she departed and went and gleaned in the field after the reapers; and she happened to come to the portion of the field belonging to Boaz, who was of the family of Elimelech.

Now behold, Boaz came from Bethlehem and said to the reapers, "May the Lord be with you." And they said to him, "May the Lord bless you." Then Boaz said to his servant who was in charge of the reapers, "Whose young woman is this?" And the servant in charge of the reapers answered and said, "She is the young Moabite woman who returned with Naomi from the land of Moab. And she said, 'Please let me glean and gather after the reapers among the sheaves.' Thus she came and has remained from the morning until now; she has been sitting in the house for a little while."

Then Boaz said to Ruth, "Listen carefully, my daughter. Do

not go to glean in another field; furthermore, do not go on from this one, but stay here with my maids. Let your eyes be on the field which they reap, and go after them. Indeed, I have commanded the servants not to touch you. When you are thirsty, go to the water jars and drink from what the servants draw."

Then she fell on her face, bowing to the ground and said to him, "Why have I found favor in your sight that you should take notice of me, since I am a foreigner?" And Boaz answered and said to her, "All that you have done for your mother-in-law after the death of your husband has been fully reported to me, and how you left your father and your mother and the land of your birth, and came to a people that you did not previously know. May the Lord reward your work, and your wages be full from the Lord, the God of Israel, under whose wings you have come to seek refuge." Then she said, "I have found favor in your sight, my lord, for you have comforted me and indeed have spoken kindly to your maidservant, though I am not like one of your maidservants."

And at mealtime Boaz said to her, "Come here, that you may eat of the bread and dip your piece of bread in the vinegar." So she sat beside the reapers; and he served her roasted grain, and she ate and was satisfied and had some left. When she rose to glean, Boaz commanded his servants, saying, "Let her glean even among the sheaves, and do not insult her. And also you shall purposely pull out for her some grain from the bundles and leave it that she may glean, and do not rebuke her."

So she gleaned in the field until evening. Then she beat out what she had gleaned, and it was about an ephah of barley. And she took it up and went into the city, and her mother-in-law saw what she had gleaned. She also took it out and gave Naomi what she had left after she was satisfied. Her mother-in-law then said to her, "Where did you glean today and where did you work? May he who took notice of you be blessed." So she told her mother-in-law with whom she had worked and said, "The name of the man with whom I worked today is Boaz." And Naomi said to her daughter-in-law, "May he be blessed of the Lord who has not withdrawn his kindness to the living and to the dead." Again Naomi said to her, "The man is our relative, he is one of our closest relatives."

Then Ruth the Moabitess said, "Furthermore, he said to me, 'You should stay close to my servants until they have finished all my harvest.' " And Naomi said to Ruth her daughter-in-law, "It is good, my daughter, that you go out with his maids, lest others fall upon you in another field." So she stayed close by the maids of Boaz in order to glean until the end of the barley harvest and the wheat harvest. And she lived with her mother-in-law.

Ruth 3:1 Then Naomi her mother-in-law said to her, "My daughter, shall I not seek security for you, that it may be well with you?"

Ruth 4:13 So Boaz took Ruth, and she became his wife, and he went in to her. And the Lord enabled her to conceive, and she gave birth to a son.

(Also read the entire Book of Ruth.)

Ruth worked without stopping, hardly allowing herself a break. Sweat trickled down her back as the sun became increasingly hot. Steadily the little heap of ears she was gleaning grew. She paused and sat down in the shade for a rest, but not for long. She wanted to surprise her mother-in-law, Naomi, with a good supply of grain.

Suddenly footsteps approached and a male voice addressed her kindly. Looking up, she saw the face of a man who was no longer young. She recognized him right away. He was the owner of the land, Boaz.

"Listen, my girl," he said. "Stay right here with us to glean; don't think of going to any other fields. Stay right behind my women workers. I have warned the young men not to bother you. When you are thirsty, go and help yourself to the water."[1]

His friendliness, care, and the warmth of his words took her by surprise. She fell to her knees, bowing. "Why are you

---

1. Ruth 2:8-9

paying attention to me?" she stammered. "You are so kind. Don't you know that I am a foreigner?"[2] *He doesn't treat me like a beggar,* she thought. *Instead, he talks to me like he would to one of his women workers who earned her own living.*

"Yes, I know," Boaz replied. "I am well aware of all that you did for your mother-in-law after the death of your husband. I also know that you left your father and your mother and your home country to live as a foreigner among our people."[3]

What a kind man, Ruth thought. She began to trust his friendliness, which she had noticed after his arrival from Bethlehem. Then she had realized that he was rich, but noticed that he treated his workers fairly and cordially. "May the Lord be with you!" he said to them, to which they had answered, "The Lord bless you!"[4] *Is this a phrase reflecting pious politeness, a way of greeting one another in this religious country?* she had wondered, *or is it the result of Boaz' close touch with God that carries over into his working relationships?*

Then Boaz spoke to her again. "The Lord recompense you for what you have done," he said, "and a full reward be given you by the Lord, the God of Israel, under whose wings you have come to take refuge."[5]

It struck Ruth how naturally he talked about God. *He does it in the same way as Naomi,* she mused. That type of relationship with God had always impressed her. *This man has indeed taken God into his considerations. I can taste that in his words and the seriousness with which he speaks. He, of all people, understands why I have come to this country. He is right. I want to find shelter under the wings of the God of Israel.*

"Your words are quite after my heart, Sir," she said simply. "You are indeed very kind to me and I am not even one of your workers."[6]

After several more hours of hard work, it was time to eat. Modestly, Ruth stayed away from the reapers. She knew her place.

2. Ruth 2:10
3. Ruth 2:11   5. Ruth 2:12
4. Ruth 2:4   6. Ruth 2:13

Once again Boaz called her to the fore. "Come up here," he called. "Eat with us."[7] After she came over, he watched personally to make sure that she received enough to eat. He cared for her till she had eaten enough.

She managed to disguise her combined fear and excitement, since she knew that Hebrew men normally had little to do with women in public, much less with a foreign woman. *Yet he is treating me like a woman of high birth, like his equal,* she thought with surprise, *even though I am a newcomer in his land.*

Ruth, whose name cannot be translated from the Hebrew because of its Moabite origins, was quickly appreciated by those around her. From the moment she set foot on Boaz' soil, she had made an impression through her loyalty, courtesy, modest manners, and desire to work. Although she was a foreigner, she could easily have made demands because of her position as daughter-in-law of the prominent Naomi. She could have pressured people for her rights under Hebrew law, which required the Israelites to help poor and foreign people.[8]

Ruth, however, didn't demand anything. She asked humbly for permission to glean ears of grain and showed deep gratitude to everyone for every favor that was extended to her. She was, furthermore, diligent in her responsibilities.

Boaz was not the only person to notice her right away; she also made a good impression on the foreman of the work crew. So in a country where it was routine for women to draw water for men, she drank from the water that the servants had drawn.

Word of her loyalty soon spread. People in Bethlehem, for example, talked about the Moabite woman who cared so well for her mother-in-law. She became known as the foreigner who had dignity, a spirit of inspiration, and concern and love toward others.

Ruth finally stopped working when evening came. After she beat out the barley she had gleaned, she had an entire bushel.

---

7. Ruth 2:14
8. Leviticus 19:9-10

Did she notice that her work in the afternoon went more smoothly than it had in the morning? Did she realize that the servants, under orders from Boaz, had snapped off some heads of barley and deliberately dropped them?

Picking up the heavy bushel, she made her way from Boaz' field to the city. Tired, satisfied, and grateful, she arrived at Naomi's.

"So much?" shouted Naomi happily when she saw how much grain Ruth was carrying. "Where have you been? For whom did you work? May God bless the man who has been so kind to you!"[9] Her questions tumbled out without stopping.

Ruth's story came out in bits and pieces. Naomi became excited about what her daughter-in-law said. She learned what had taken place that day. She heard all about what Boaz had said and done and how Ruth had been personally invited to keep coming back to glean till all the field had been harvested.

"Why, that man is one of our closest relatives," Naomi exclaimed after she had heard the whole story.[10] Surprise rang in her voice, and hope. She was impressed that God had led Ruth so clearly from the very first day. Boaz was a link with the past. Would he also become a bridge to a new future?

Throughout the following weeks, Ruth went to the field every morning till the barley and wheat harvests were over. Although she had gleaned enough food on that first day to last her for weeks, she did not slow down. She never made claims to the fact that she was related to rich Boaz. Fulfilling her tasks without pretensions, she was faithful to the given promise that she wouldn't leave Naomi alone.

Six or eight weeks passed by swiftly and, as usual, all the workers celebrated the end of the harvest season with an elaborate meal. After eating and drinking his fill, Boaz lay down to sleep on the threshing floor in order to keep watch over his grain.

This was the ideal situation that Naomi had been waiting for.[11] According to Hebrew law, a widow without children

9. Ruth 2:19
10. Ruth 2:20
11. Ruth 3:2

had the right of a levirate marriage. In order to keep the name of a deceased husband intact, Moses had instituted that the brother who was next to the dead husband in age should then marry the widow. The first son born out of that marriage would then continue the original family line of the deceased so that his name would not be forgotten.[12]

In order to keep a family's property intact, a law of redemption was established. Under this law, property sold by a poor man would be bought by a close relative. If the man had no relatives, he could sell the land to anyone but was expected to buy it back when he had money. If he remained poor, the land would automatically revert back to him during the Year of Jubilee which came every 50 years.

As far as Naomi knew, Boaz was the closest relative with whom Ruth could claim her rights, for Elimelech had no living brothers. But Naomi was not only mindful of the continuation of the name and descendants of her husband and sons; she was also interested in Ruth's happiness. She had watched the course of events of the past weeks carefully and could not help but clearly see God's leading in them.

She and Ruth had arrived in Bethlehem at the beginning of the two harvests. Without even knowing it, Ruth had gone straight to the land of Boaz. And, of course, even as an outsider she had immediately detected the first signs of kindled love. These seemed to be signs that God was using the circumstances to bring Ruth and Boaz together.

Naomi also recognized similarities between the relationship Ruth and Boaz had and the marriages of her prominent ancestors. Since his mother was also a non-Israelite woman,[13] Boaz seemed to be a suitable husband for Ruth. She in turn would be a good helper for him. This was the norm God had established for Eve, the first woman.[14]

Aspects of their relationship also turned Naomi's thoughts back to the Patriarch Abraham and his wife, Sarah. And, like the wives of Isaac and Jacob—Rebekah and Rachel—Ruth's desire to work diligently had developed into contact with a godly man. Undoubtedly the love of the man for the woman, which had formed the seal of those earlier covenants,[15] was also present in Boaz.

The next thing Naomi had to do was check whether God

12. Deuteronomy 25:5-10   14. Genesis 2:18
13. Joshua 6:25; Matthew 1:5 15. Genesis 24:67; 29:20

was opening or closing doors. So she came up with a proposal based on three factors: fulfillment of God's laws, her love for Ruth, and her perception of the Holy Spirit's leading.

"Take a bath, use some perfume, and put on a nice dress. Then go to the threshing floor tonight," she said. "Be sure that Boaz doesn't notice you before he has finished his supper. Watch where he lies down to sleep and then quietly lie down at his feet. After that he will make it clear what you have to do further."[16]

Ruth, schooled in the Moabite culture, thought that this was a strange suggestion. She was willing to follow Israelite law, but she was a modest woman; she was also high-spirited and dared to make far-reaching decisions. Above all, she loved chastity and purity.

But she also had a deep respect for Naomi and believed that Naomi would do anything she could to make her happy. She knew that Naomi would not make a wrong proposal and would not suggest anything dishonorable. She knew that Naomi reckoned with God and it would be wise to listen to her advice.

"Your God shall be my God, your people shall be my people," Ruth had declared to Naomi on the road to Bethlehem.[17] Now it was time to adapt herself to the laws of this land and the God in whom she had taken refuge. He would watch over her. He would not forsake her, even now. Trusting Him, she decided to do what Naomi had proposed.

Ruth also had a deep respect for Boaz. He was the man who, without her even asking, had proven to be her protector and provider. Hadn't he already shown that he understood her? He was a man who walked closely with God. He wouldn't hurt her or cause her pain.

"I will do what you suggest," she answered Naomi.[18] That night she lay down at Boaz' feet, a woman who once again had adorned herself as a bride for a man. She waited expectantly, wondering how Boaz would react.

Around midnight Boaz woke up and was startled to find a woman lying at his feet. Ruth then told him her story,

16. Ruth 3:3-4
17. Ruth 1:16
18. Ruth 3:5

simply and clearly. "On the basis of God's law, I ask that I may be your wife, for you are my closest relative."[19]

Boaz' reaction touched her deeply. He showed again how much he understood her. She was moved by his humility.

Overlooking the fact that he himself was a desirable suitor, Boaz talked about Ruth's faithfulness to her deceased husband. He touched on her purity in dealing with men and praised her virtues that were known to everyone in the city.

He continued by saying that he was willing to marry her. There was a problem, however, for another man was more closely related to Ruth than he was. If that man waived his rights by not redeeming her, then the way was free for him. Through this test, God would clearly show which of the two men He intended to be Ruth's husband.

Ruth didn't need to go through the trying experience of offering herself once again to a man. Boaz would arrange that for her. Once more he showed his concern for her. He would not send her away in the middle of the night.

Early in the morning while it was still dark, Ruth left Boaz and went out into the empty streets. Boaz had not touched her. His deep love and respect for her had been expressed through his control over his desires.

He had also protected her good name. No one would need to know that she had been on the threshing floor. If this fact should ever become known, it would damage her reputation and she would not be a suitable partner for a redeemer.

Boaz not only guarded himself against evil; he was also conscious of the ideas other people might have. His conversation and attitude proved that God was foremost in his thoughts.

Ruth walked quietly through the city, thinking. *It is just like the first time I met him. Then it was during an orderly working day but now it has been an unexpected situation at night.* Now she was sure that Boaz was close to God and knew in her heart that she could entrust herself to such a man.

19. Ruth 3:9

As she was leaving, Boaz had handed her a bushel and a half of barley. "You should not arrive at your mother-in-law's emptyhanded," he had said.[20] By this act, Boaz communicated two promises to Ruth. When he married her, he would not forget Naomi. He also pledged, in view of their future marriage, a small portion of her bridal gift. If for some reason Ruth would meet someone on her way home, this token of his care for her would serve as a reasonable explanation for her early morning walk.

Boaz, whose name may have meant "fleetness," lived up to his name. That very day he settled all necessary details according to the rules of the law.[21] Energetically he met with the other relative—the potential redeemer of Ruth—at the gate of the city. Then he called together 10 elders of the city and held a meeting. After the other man decided not to marry Ruth because such a marriage might jeopardize his inheritance, Boaz bought Naomi's land before witnesses. This made him responsible for the inheritance of her husband and her sons. He became Ruth's legal husband and promised that a future son would carry the family name of her first husband.

The bride was a woman of exceptional qualities. She was brave, having dared to exchange a well-known present for an unknown future. She was stalwart and had developed initiative, but at the same time was willing to listen to others' advice. She was loyal and kept her promises. Industrious, humble, and pure, she was known throughout the city for her radiating love. The bridegroom had undivided attention for her. He respected her femininity highly. Because of his love, he protected and cared for her.

A remarkable relationship based on understanding existed between the two partners. They could talk with one another and knew how to listen. Lack of communication—the dangerous rock on which many marriages are broken up—did not threaten them. Their mutual respect and desire to further the other's interests guaranteed a happy marriage. This marriage had the characteristics of a covenant made in heaven.

20. Ruth 3:15
21. Ruth 4:1-10

Ruth, the woman who loved God and her fellowmen, experienced God's favor. Her son, Obed, was chosen by Him to become a forefather in the lineage of Jesus, the Messiah.[22] The privilege every Hebrew woman was hoping for was extended to her. She became a mother in the line of the Redeemer.

A mile east of Bethlehem stands the "field of Boaz," which is known as the spot where Ruth gleaned ears of corn. The field next to it is called the "field of the shepherds." Tradition holds that the angels first proclaimed Christ's birth over that spot. In the place where the love between Ruth and Boaz started to blossom, angels over a thousand years later sang, "Glory to God in the highest, and on earth peace among men with whom He is pleased!" (Luke 2:14)

The Bible contains two books named after women: Ruth and Esther. Having great respect for both books, the Jews read the Book of Esther at the Feast of Purim and the Scroll of Ruth at the Feast of Pentecost.

Christians the world over should gratefully recognize Ruth's contribution. The Messiah, the redeemer of Israel, is also the Saviour of the world. Through Ruth, Hebrew and Christian are forever united. Ruth's influence, far from being restricted to the Hebrew land and people, permeates human history up to the present day.

Ruth, a woman characterized by loyalty
(Ruth 2:1-23; 3:1; 4:13; also read the entire Book of Ruth.)

Questions:
1. What aspect of Ruth's life had the greatest influence?
2. Why do you believe Ruth's life took such a favorable turn?
3. List Ruth's virtues and underline the most important ones for you.
4. Study her relationship with Boaz thoughtfully. Do you think they were led to one another by God? If so, why? Do you see the foundation of a happy marriage in this story? Describe your reason(s).

22. Matthew 1:5

5. What encouragement can people who experience mourning and sorrow draw from Ruth's life?
6. Summarize the principles that you have learned from Ruth. Consider prayerfully which of these you should apply in your life right now.

*"The safe way for any marriage—as for any human
relationship—is the shared experience of God.
We can disagree on any number of other things
and keep on loving, if we agree about God."**

Eugenia Price

Michal,
a woman whose marriage lacked unity
and fell apart

1 Samuel 19:10-17 And Saul tried to pin David to the wall with
the spear, but he slipped away out of Saul's presence, so
that he struck the spear into the wall. And David fled and escaped that night. Then Saul sent messengers to David's
house to watch him, in order to put him to death in the morning. But Michal, David's wife, told him, saying, "If you do not
save your life tonight, tomorrow you will be put to death." So
Michal let David down through a window, and he went out
and fled and escaped. And Michal took the household idol
and laid it on the bed, and put a quilt of goats' hair at its
head, and covered it with clothes.

When Saul sent messengers to take David, she said, "He
is sick." Then Saul sent messengers to see David, saying,
"Bring him up to me on his bed, that I may put him to death."
When the messengers entered, behold, the household idol
was on the bed with the quilt of goats' hair at its head. So
Saul said to Michal, "Why have you deceived me like this and
let my enemy go, so that he has escaped?" And Michal said
to Saul, "He said to me, 'Let me go! Why should I put you to
death?' "

*From *The Unique World of Women* by Eugenia Price, page 76. Copyright ©
1969 by Zondervan Publishing House. Used by permission.

2 Samuel 6:16-23 Then it happened as the ark of the Lord came into the city of David that Michal the daughter of Saul looked out of the window and saw King David leaping and dancing before the Lord; and she despised him in her heart. So they brought in the ark of the Lord and set it in its place inside the tent which David had pitched for it; and David offered burnt offerings and peace offerings before the Lord. And when David had finished offering the burnt offering and the peace offering, he blessed the people in the name of the Lord of hosts. Further, he distributed to all the people, to all the multitude of Israel, both to men and women, a cake of bread and one of dates and one of raisins to each one. Then all the people departed each to his house.

But when David returned to bless his household, Michal the daughter of Saul came out to meet David and said, "How the king of Israel distinguished himself today! He uncovered himself today in the eyes of his servants' maids as one of the foolish ones shamelessly uncovers himself!"

So David said to Michal, "It was before the Lord, who chose me above your father and above all his house, to appoint me ruler over the people of the Lord, over Israel; therefore I will celebrate before the Lord. And I will be more lightly esteemed than this and will be humble in my own eyes, but with the maids of whom you have spoken, with them I will be distinguished." And Michal the daughter of Saul had no child to the day of her death.

The marriage of Michal, the youngest daughter of King Saul, did not enjoy a happy start. The marriage problems had not developed due to the difference in social standing between the king's daughter and the shepherd boy. Rather, Saul had arranged David's marriage to Michal hoping that it would make him unhappy and cause his death.[1] Saul had given his daughter to David in marriage because he wanted David to die.

Saul could no longer stand the man who would become king in his place, the man who had already won the love of his people. On many occasions he had already tried to kill David, though without success.

---

1. 1 Samuel 18:17-21

David, in fact, had earned the right to marry Saul's eldest daughter, Merab. The king had promised her to the man who would defeat the Philistine Goliath.[2] But the king had not kept his promise. By the time David was ready to marry Merab, the king had given her to someone else.[3]

Then Saul offered his youngest daughter, Michal, to David on the condition that David would kill 100 Philistines. *The possibility that David could hold out against that many Philistines is so small,* the king thought grimly, *that he will surely lose his life.*

But Saul had excluded God from his thinking. Through God's blessing, the young man killed 200 Philistines and Michal became his wife.[4]

It is no wonder that Michal loved David. He was handsome, courageous, but also sensitive. Next to being a brave warrior, he was an artistic man who wrote songs and composed music. He was popular with the people and had been appointed to be their next king. The most striking characteristic of David's life, however, was his relationship with God. This relationship gave him a certain charm which, though not always definable, was clearly present.

Soon it became clear that David's being Saul's son-in-law had not changed the king's feelings. Again Saul began brooding about how he could take David's life. When he discovered that he could not get rid of David through war or his own weapon, he devised a plan to kill David in his own house.

Michal, however, heard about the plot. "If you don't get away quickly," she warned David, "you are a dead man."[5] Thus she helped her husband escape in time. When the servants of her father came the next day to fetch him, he was gone. "He is sick," Michal lied,[6] probably to win time.

That was the last drop in Saul's cup of fury. "Then bring him in his bed anyway," he commanded angrily.[7] Soon he discovered that his daughter had deceived him. A disguised house-god had been placed in the bed to look like David. It is uncertain whether David knew that this idol was in his home. But it was the first indication of a growing breach

---

2. 1 Samuel 17:25
3. 1 Samuel 18:19
4. 1 Samuel 18:27

5. 1 Samuel 19:11
6. 1 Samuel 19:14
7. 1 Samuel 19:15

between Michal and her godly husband.

Outwardly, their marriage seemed to have spiritual unity. Michal worshiped the God of Israel just like her husband. But in her heart that God was a stranger to her; her relationship was not one of trusting Him. Her husband, on the other hand, did not worship other gods; his love for God was undivided and applied to daily situations.

The only foundation on which anyone can build is Jesus Christ (1 Corinthians 3:11). The annual reports of the Help-by-Telephone services in Holland illustrate this point. Of those needing help, the people with marital problems belonged to the largest group and every year the number is increasing at an alarming rate.

Lack of spiritual unity in a marriage initially might seem to be only a scratch on marital happiness. But such a scratch often becomes a crack, which then widens into a gulf that cannot be bridged. The mutual life-house cannot be built on an uneven foundation. Such a marriage from the beginning lacks the solid base it needs to be happy and durable enough to survive the storms that are bound to come. No right-thinking person would risk moving into a house that either has no foundation at all, or that is built on a weak one. So it is unthinkable that the highly important choice of finding a life-partner so often is done without consideration of spiritual principles which can stand firm against life's strains.

When her father furiously accused her, "Why have you deceived me and let my enemy escape?" Michal replied, "He threatened to kill me if I didn't help him."[8]

These were revealing words. Instead of speaking the truth, Michal accused David in a terrible way. The man who before long would refuse to avenge himself on his father-in-law, the man whose conscience would disturb him when he only cut off the edge of Saul's robe, and who would restrain his men from killing his pursuer,[9] was here charged with an attempt to murder his wife.

Michal's acts differed greatly from David's. In the same situation, David threw himself upon his God, something he always did in trying circumstances. God was his refuge and he expected the solutions to his problems to come from

8. 1 Samuel 19:17
9. 1 Samuel 24:1-7

Him. Indeed, David's line of thought was completely opposite to his wife's unbelief and deceitful spirit.

The spiritual rift between David and Michal was becoming obvious. But what had happened also put a question mark on Michal's professed love.

David and Michal clearly traveled different roads. Predictably, after David's disappearance their marriage terminated abruptly. The cause was not, however, due to the absence of spiritual unity. In his desire to get revenge on David, Saul gave his daughter to another man in marriage—to Palti, the son of Laish, of Gallim.[10]

Paul wrote in his letter to the Corinthians that the difference between a Christian and a non-Christian can be compared to the contrast between righteousness and gross injustice, light and darkness (2 Corinthians 6:14-15). God's love demonstrated through a Christian is patient and kind, humble and unselfish. It is happy when truth wins out and avoids trouble at all costs (1 Corinthians 6:4-6).

Years passed, and after David became king over Judah he called for Michal to return to him. What moved him to call for her?[11] The Bible is not explicit. Also, no mention is made of the feelings of Michal, who like a handball had been thrown from one man to another. No doubt her emotions were torn as she left her second husband and watched him weep in anguish as she slowly returned to David.

After this incident, we meet Michal one more time. Again years have passed, for David is now king over all of Israel. He had experienced the glorious high-point of his life. God had fulfilled His promises. His enemies were defeated and his kingship was highly respected among the surrounding nations.[12]

Yet, the crown on David's work was still to come. He had one more service to do for God. It was impossible for David to be happy until the ark—the proof of God's presence—arrived at its rightful place in Jerusalem, the capital.

When that day finally came, the whole of Jerusalem streamed together to receive the ark of the Lord in a festive manner and to bring it to the place David had appointed for it. The priests and the Levites had prepared themselves spiritually for their tasks. The singers and the musicians

10. 1 Samuel 25:44
11. 2 Samuel 3:14-15
12. 1 Chronicles 14:2

already had tuned their instruments. The leaders of the people had taken their places in the procession and were joined by many from the population of Israel.

Suddenly an indescribable shout of rejoicing broke loose. Cymbals, trumpets, harps, and zithers competed with the voices of the people in praising God.[13]

The happiest person of all was King David. A deep gratitude swelled in his heart; God was allowing him this honor. David experienced the occasion—not as the proud king—but as a sinful person who was aware of the presence of a holy God.

In this situation, it was fitting that he put aside his royal robe and gird himself with the linen breeches that God had ordered priests to war.[14] The great king rightly felt that he could only appear before God in the dress of a servant of the ark. He didn't merely want to be the peoples' authority, a man who blessed them with fatherly presents. He sought to identify himself with them. Before God, he was their equal, equally judged by Him. Their God was his God.

David then expressed his overwhelming joy and thankfulness in a religious dance. This dance, modeled after Eastern custom, visually demonstrated his feelings toward God.

Michal was missing from the crowd which moved out to receive the ark festively. Once again it became evident how great the breach between her and David really was. Michal didn't share the religious convictions of her husband. This great day, a highlight in his life, didn't impress her in the least. Like her father, Michal was not concerned about the ark of God.[15] She felt no desire to fetch a tambourine and lead the women in a song to the Lord as Miriam once had.[16]

Quite the contrary. Michal despised David because of his excitement and actions. From behind a window, she watched him at a distance as he danced among the common people. In her heart, she looked down on him.

When David returned home after the arrival of the ark, desirous to share the joy of the day's festivities with Michal, she approached him with a scornful, biting remark. "How

---

13. 1 Chronicles 15:3-25
14. Exodus 28:42-43; 1 Samuel 2:18
15. 1 Chronicles 13:3
16. Exodus 15:20-21

glorious the king of Israel looked today!" she sneered. "He exposed himself to the girls along the street like a common pervert!"[17]

These words did not express thoughts about God. Michal despised the king, her husband, who could forget himself in such a way to identify himself humbly with his people. She had only biting sarcasm for a man who, in her opinion, had thrown his dignity away.

Michal was proud and cold of heart—toward God, toward her people, toward her husband. In her sarcasm she called David perverse and impudent. Not only did she reject his religion, she besmirched it. She called it immorality. Once again, Michal placed David in an unfavorable light.

The absence of love painfully revealed itself. Michal not only did not love her husband and her husband's God, but also lacked the love of one person for another. After many years of marriage, she still did not know her husband's heart. She did not consider the things that moved him. His motives were not hers.

Man has been created in the image of God (Genesis 1:26) and as such should be approached with dignity.

The widening gap between husband and wife was not due primarily to differences of character or ambition. Rather, each thought and responded out of different religious frameworks. Her husband's obvious fear of the Lord had not kindled a desire in Michal's heart to experience the Lord God in the same way. Their many years of marriage had not touched her inner person spiritually.

Michal did not become a wife after David's heart because she was not a woman after God's heart. David felt closer to the simple women among the people—who loved God—than he did to his own wife.

The Bible does not record how long Michal lived after this incident, but it does imply that her married life was over. The rift between the partners was now complete.

"Michal, the daughter of Saul, had no child to the day of her death," says the Bible.[18] Those few words reveal God's disapproval of a woman who treated the man after His heart[19] badly. He kept her from having children. The con-

17. 2 Samuel 6:20
18. 2 Samuel 6:23
19. Acts 13:22

clusion could also be drawn that after this incident David no longer went to Michal as her husband. Her external role as his wife was over, and she spent the remainder of her days in loneliness. She died without having an influence and may never have met the God of her husband through personal commitment.

The marriage of David and Michal stands as a warning in history. If a husband and wife are not one in God—sharing spiritual unity—their marriage-union may fold under life's pressures.

Michal,
a woman whose marriage lacked unity and fell apart
(1 Samuel 19:10-17; 2 Samuel 6:16-23)

Questions:
1. Study the marriage of David and Michal carefully and list their differences.
2. Consider this list in view of 2 Corinthians 6:14-15. What do you believe was the greatest difference between them?
3. We read in 1 Samuel 18:20, 28 that before their marriage Michal loved David. During their life together did Michal really love him in light of the Bible's definition of love? (1 Corinthians 13:4-7)
4. Read 1 Samuel 19:13-17 and Psalm 59 and compare David's and Michal's relationships to God.
5. What basic principles of marriage have you learned through this story?
6. In what ways can you apply the principles of loyalty and commitment (or lack thereof) studied in this story to your own life?

14

"A woman's inner beauty is almost always dependent upon her relationship with God."*

Eugenia Price

Abigail,
a woman who watched over the
conscience of a servant of God

1 Samuel 25:23-42 When Abigail saw David, she hurried and dismounted from her donkey, and fell on her face before David, and bowed herself to the ground. And she fell at his feet and said, "On me alone, my lord, be the blame. And please let your maidservant speak to you, and listen to the words of your maidservant. Please do not let my lord pay attention to this worthless man, Nabal, for as his name is, so is he. Nabal is his name and folly is with him; but I your maidservant did not see the young men of my lord whom you sent.

"Now therefore, my lord, as the Lord lives, and as your soul lives, since the Lord has restrained you from shedding blood, and from avenging yourself by your own hand, now then let your enemies, and those who seek evil against my lord, be as Nabal. And now let this gift which your maidservant has brought to my lord be given to the young men who accompany my lord. Please forgive the transgression of your maidservant; for the Lord will certainly make for my lord an enduring house, because my lord is fighting the battles of the Lord, and evil shall not be found in you all your days. And

---

*From *The Unique World of Women* by Eugenia Price, page 82. Copyright © 1969 by Zondervan Publishing House. Used by permission.

should anyone rise up to pursue you and to seek your life, then the life of my lord shall be bound in the bundle of the living with the Lord your God; but the lives of your enemies He will sling out as from the hollow of a sling.

"And it shall come about when the Lord shall do for my lord according to all the good that He has spoken concerning you, and shall appoint you ruler over Israel, that this will not cause grief or a troubled heart to my lord, both by having shed blood without cause and by my lord having avenged himself. When the Lord shall deal well with my lord, then remember your maidservant."

Then David said to Abigail, "Blessed be the Lord God of Israel, who sent you this day to meet me, and blessed be your discernment, and blessed be you, who have kept me this day from bloodshed, and from avenging myself by my own hand. Nevertheless, as the Lord God of Israel lives, who has restrained me from harming you, unless you had come quickly to meet me, surely there would not have been left to Nabal until the morning light as much as one male."

So David received from her hand what she had brought him, and he said to her, "Go up to your house in peace. See, I have listened to you and granted your request." Then Abigail came to Nabal, and behold, he was holding a feast in his house, like the feast of a king. And Nabal's heart was merry within him, for he was very drunk; so she did not tell him anything at all until the morning light. But it came about in the morning, when the wine had gone out of Nabal, that his wife told him these things, and his heart died within him so that he became as a stone. About ten days later, it happened that the Lord struck Nabal, and he died.

When David heard that Nabal was dead, he said, "Blessed be the Lord, who has pleaded the cause of my reproach from the hand of Nabal, and has kept back His servant from evil. The Lord has also returned the evil doing of Nabal on his own head." Then David sent a proposal to Abigail, to take her as his wife. When the servants of David came to Abigail at Carmel, they spoke to her, saying, "David has sent us to you, to take you as his wife." And she arose and bowed with her face to the ground and said, "Behold, your maidservant is a maid to wash the feet of my lord's servants." Then Abigail quickly arose, and rode on a donkey, with her five

maidens who attended her; and she followed the
messengers of David, and became his wife.

Her hands moved quickly.
Her thoughts ran even faster.
Although she realized that the situation was serious,
Abigail did not panic or become nervous. Calmly she made
her plans. She did not forget that she was pressed for time,
that she could not lose one second.
The words of the servant a few moments ago kept resound-
ing in her ears. "Know well what you have to do, madam,"
the servant had said, "for there is going to be great trouble
ahead, for our master, for all of us. I am coming to you
because the boss is such a stubborn lout that no one can
even talk to him."[1]
Because the situation was so extremely serious[2] and there
was no room for error, Abigail was handling everything
herself. She didn't dare to leave such responsibilities to her
servants.
She had to think quickly and accurately. What would 600
ravenous men, living in the rough outdoors, need to still
their hunger? Thus she came to a respectable provisioning,
having gathered enough food to satisfy all those men.
Abigail did not only think of the most necessary essen-
tials, such as bread and meat. She also packed measures of
roasted grain, 200 clusters of raisins, delicious fig cakes,
and two jugs of wine.[3] She wanted to take good care of
the men, and desired to bring them into a favorable mood.
In a minimum of time everything was taken care of ef-
ficiently. "Go on ahead of me," she ordered the servants. "I
will follow you."[4] Psychologically, it was a tactical move.
Abigail's servants could start their work before she herself
arrived.
She didn't talk to her husband, Nabal, about her plans,
knowing that her words wouldn't penetrate his drunken
stupor.
Nabal had arranged a great feast to celebrate his annual

1. 1 Samuel 25:17   3. 1 Samuel 25:18
2. 1 Samuel 25:1-22   4. 1 Samuel 25:19

shearing of sheep. He was a wealthy man, possessing 3,000 sheep and 1,000 goats. The shearing of sheep was important, for wool was a vital commodity in the culture of Canaan.

After the extensive work was finished, Nabal offered the shearers—experts who were specially hired for this job—a meal. And the noisiest man at the table was Nabal himself.

Abigail's husband was the descendant of a great man, Caleb.[5] But he in no way resembled his illustrious forefather, who had excelled in the fear of God, insight, and courage. Nabal, whose name meant "the fool," was precisely that—a rude, clumsy fellow who failed to talk reasonably.

That was what David experienced when, through his messengers, he asked Nabal for food for himself and his 600 followers. It was a normal request, for David and his men had formed a wall of protection around Nabal's shearers of sheep to keep robbers and roving nomads from harming them during their work. Any Arab sheik—even today—could have asked for the same treatment and not have been rejected.

David had made his request modestly. He had approached Nabal in a submissive manner and talked to him like a son would to his father. In spite of David's tactful approach, Nabal's reaction was rude and insulting. "Who is this fellow David?" he had snorted. "Who does this son of Jesse think he is? There are lots of servants these days who run away from their masters. Should I take my bread and my water and my meat that I have slaughtered for my shearers and give it to a gang who suddenly appears from nowhere?"[6]

This answer was extremely offensive to David, who was popular throughout the entire country. Women from all the towns of Israel had been singing about his victories,[7] and he had already been anointed to be the next king. Even Nabal's servants praised him for his help and for the way he disciplined his men.[8] He had demonstrated prudent and strong leadership, keeping his soldiers—who had few means of ex-

5. 1 Samuel 25:3; Numbers 14:6-10, 24   7. 1 Samuel 18:6-7
6. 1 Samuel 25:10-11   8. 1 Samuel 25:15-16

istence—organized and responsive to his commands.

In spite of these factors, Nabal treated David like an insignificant man, a rebel whose requests you do not need to take into serious consideration.

David reacted to this scornful treatment with an outburst of rage. Only recently he had refused to avenge himself on Saul, who had tried to kill him, and had left the matter for God to judge.[9] During his fight with the insulting and cursing giant Goliath, he had thought only of the name of his God.[10] The man who later in history would be known as "a man after God's heart"[11] could not ignore this personal insult. He wanted to take immediate revenge.

"Gird your sword, every one of you," he commanded. "No male in Nabal's house will remain alive. By tomorrow morning we will be finished with every one of them."[12] To avenge himself of Nabal's insult, David started on his way to the shepherd's home with 400 men.

Abigail, meanwhile, mounted a donkey and rode to meet David. A woman who was humble enough to listen to the advice of a servant, she had enough character and courage to face David's anger. She was high-spirited, attractive, intelligent, and wise. Although the meaning of her name was "My Father [God] gives joy," it did not reflect her present circumstances, chained as she was by her marriage to Nabal. It can only be vaguely guessed what living with such a foolish brute had meant for such a believing and sensitive woman.

This certainly was not the first time that Abigail had tried to glue together the pieces her husband had broken. When she met David, her words proved that. "It is entirely my fault, Sir," she said. "I didn't see the messengers you sent."[13] In other words she was saying, "If I had seen them, I would have used my influence to prevent this trouble."

Abigail's attitude was both tactful and impressive. Although she truthfully called her husband a bad-tempered fool, yet she identified with him in acknowledging fault. In her attitude and resultant actions, she followed the same principle other great men in God's kingdom would follow.

9. 1 Samuel 24:5-7
10. 1 Samuel 17:45-47
11. Acts 13:22
12. 1 Samuel 25:13, 22
13. 1 Samuel 25:25

Nehemiah[14] and Daniel,[15] for example, would later identify with the guilt of the Jewish people who were disobedient to God. Abigail asked no forgiveness for Nabal; she only requested it for herself.

Abigail's attitude, as well as her words, impressed David. As soon as the two groups met on the trail and Abigail saw David, she quickly dismounted. She bowed low before him out of respect. The future king of Israel and a servant of God who had been ignored by her husband as an unworthy person now received her honor. The men on whom Nabal didn't want to waste water received wine offered to them by his wife.

Solomon later remarked that a gift makes room for a person, and brings him in the presence of great men.[16] Abigail experienced that lesson. The presents she sent ahead had softened David's heart and cooled off his fury. Her appearance and her words now could do the rest.

What she continued to say showed such exceptional wisdom and insight that it can best be described with what James later in the New Testament called the "wisdom from above." Such wisdom is "first pure, then peaceable, gentle, open to reason, full of mercy and good fruits, without uncertainty or insincerity."[17]

The most impressive thing about Abigail was that she did not exhibit a false front. She was seen as she really was. The circumstances had not allowed her time to reflect thoroughly about the situation beforehand. There had been no time to gather strength, courage, or wisdom. There had been no time for intellectual or spiritual bravado. She could not pretend to be different than she was, for the storms of life blow away any cover from a person that is not an integral part of himself. His immediate reactions then become the garb in which he is seen.

This was Abigail's attitude toward the holy God. Her heart trembled before Him. She loved Him above everything else, and was convinced that above all else a human being had to consider Him. Nobody, she knew, should try to deceive Him. He could not be deceived, and

14. Nehemiah 1:4-11   16. Proverbs 18:16
15. Daniel 9:3-19   17. James 3:17

the consequences of such an attempt would be painful.

God had blessed David abundantly. Suddenly, as she faced him, Abigail saw that the blessings David had already experienced would be small compared to what the Lord was still planning to do for the future king.

From her deep respect for God, Abigail had gleaned a love for His servant, for this fellow human being. Her love was pure, sincere, and spontaneous. Through her reliance on God, Abigail also maintained a proper attitude toward herself. Instead of being self-centered, she was modest and avoided self-pity.

Although tactfully trying to save the lives of Nabal and his men, she seemed to be driven by a deeper motive. She was thinking about those who in this situation were threatened by desire for revenge. In blind fury, David and his men were about to commit a sin that they would always regret. The crime he was about to commit would be irreparable. A heavy weight would burden his conscience the rest of his days. The stain of blood from both the innocent and the guilty would be on his hands.

Abigail reminded David of the favor of God that he was enjoying, the special protection he was experiencing. She drew his attention to the privileged future awaiting him under the blessed hand of God as Israel's future king. David's name was connected with the name of God. Through his rejection of David, Nabal had dishonored God's name. But the future king was also on the brink of putting an indelible disgrace on that name. In a quick-tempered thirst for blood, he was willing to take his rights into his own hands and kill innocent people.

Abigail was convinced that God would punish Nabal for his impertinence toward His anointed one. But she knew that He did not need David to execute judgment. She didn't reprove David. She only painted the consequences of his rash decision, beginning her plea with the words, "As the Lord lives."[18] She did this with such natural eloquence that the poet David found it hard not to be fascinated by her style of delivery.

18. 1 Samuel 25:26

In his letter to the Corinthians, Paul wrote that every Christian should seek the good of his neighbor (1 Corinthians 10:24) and should avoid being offensive to anyone (1 Corinthians 10:32).

Abigail was God-centered. She put God first in her thoughts and exemplified Him in everything she said. She was not only thinking about the lives of her husband and his workers; she was also mindful of David's reputation. She saw things in light of the future plans God had laid out for him. Her plea, therefore, was based on what was best for David and not on her own interests. Her motivating force was love for David as her fellowman.

What Abigail was hoping for happened. David's conscience awakened. Her appeal based on God's character and sovereign power disarmed him. "Bless the Lord God of Israel who has sent you to meet me today!" David exclaimed. "Thank God for your good sense! Bless you for keeping me from murdering the men and carrying vengeance with my own hands. For I swear by the Lord, the God of Israel who has kept me from hurting you, that if you had not come out to meet me, not one of Nabal's men would be alive tomorrow morning."[19]

With these words, David thanked the woman who had watched over his conscience and kept him from sin and remorse. Because of her direct, spiritual approach to the problem, he discovered how clouded his own view was, how self-centered he had been because of his personal involvement. David then reestablished a proper sight on God, who through this woman had kept him from making a terrible mistake.

Abigail, who fully realized the extent and the far-reaching results of David's plan, consequently acted with wisdom and insight. She not only prevented a man from becoming a murderer, but saved the reputation of a future king. David, a man so highly respected that future generations would refer to Jesus Christ as "the Son of David," did not lose his self-respect. He conquered his anger and through self-control won a greater victory than the control of a city.[20]

Most important of all, however, was the fact that David

19. 1 Samuel 25:32-34
20. Proverbs 16:32

didn't sin against the Lord. He did not give God a reason to sorrow. God's enemies did not get a chance to slander His holy name. "Go back in peace to your house. See, I have listened to your words, and I have granted your request."[21] Those were his parting words to Abigail.

Abigail had viewed the situation correctly. Things did turn out badly for Nabal. When he heard from his wife the next morning what had happened the previous day, his reaction of fury and fright resulted in a stroke. He died 10 days later, experiencing in his body the lesson that no one can scoff at God and remain unpunished.

"For the reverence and fear of God are basic to all wisdom," wrote Solomon. "Knowing God results in every other kind of understanding (Proverbs 9:10, The Living Bible). When we revere and trust the Lord, we may be taught by Him (Proverbs 1:7). Since His wisdom is so closely related to knowing and obeying His Word, we must intensely examine Scripture as if we were searching for an earthly treasure. God will then reward us with the wisdom we are seeking (Proverbs 2:1-6).

When David heard that Nabal had died, he praised and thanked God for paying Nabal back.[22] God had kept him from taking matters into his own hands. David then showed what an unforgettable impression Abigail had made on him. Right away, without wasting a minute, he asked her to become his wife and Abigail gladly agreed.

Abigail's petition, "When the Lord has done these great things for you, please remember me!"[23] received surprising fulfillment. She knew from experience how great a loneliness there could be within a marriage where the partners had little in common. But she now became the wife of a man with whom she shared many things: courage, faithfulness, an active intellect, and discretionary insight.

David and Abigail's greatest unity, however, lay in their attitudes toward God. He had first place in both their hearts. Abigail, the unselfish one, experienced how God could work all things together for good for those who love Him.[24] She had unexpectedly become a wife of the king of Israel. Unfortunately, Abigail was only one of David's eight wives.[25] Following the example of the other royal courts of his time, David had not restricted himself to the monogamous marriage covenant given by God.

21. 1 Samuel 25:35
22. 1 Samuel 25:39
23. 1 Samuel 25:31
24. Romans 8:28
25. 2 Samuel 3:2-5, 13; 11:26-27

Abigail's attitude toward God, her respect for her fellow-man, and her modest thinking prevented one of the greatest men in history from dragging his name in the dirt.

Through Abigail's keen insight and wise approach to a difficult situation, David received the opportunity to remain before God as he was, the man after God's own heart. He was still able to fulfill the purpose for which he and every human being had been created: to bring honor to the name of God.[26] As the future king, he would have missed that chance completely had not a woman come into his life at the right time and watched over his conscience, thus preventing him from insulting God.

Abigail, a woman who watched over the conscience of a servant of God.
(1 Samuel 25:23-42)

Questions:
1. List several of Abigail's most important characteristics.
2. What impresses you when you examine her attitude toward Nabal?
3. What proves that Abigail possessed "wisdom from above"? (James 3:17)
4. Solomon has much to say about becoming wise (Proverbs 1:7; 2:1-6; 9:10). What are the steps necessary to acquire wisdom?
5. What possibilities to gain godly wisdom do we have in our time that Abigail was missing?
6. What is the most important principle you have learned from this woman? How will it influence your life?

15

*"Therefore murder shall be a constant threat
in your family from this time on, because you
have insulted Me by taking Uriah's wife."**
Nathan

Bathsheba,
a woman who did not prevent a God-
fearing man from insulting his God

2 Samuel 11:1-17, 26-27 Then it happened in the spring, at
the time when kings go out to battle, that David sent Joab
and his servants with him and all Israel, and they destroyed
the sons of Ammon and besieged Rabbah. But David stayed
at Jerusalem. Now when evening came David arose from his
bed and walked around on the roof of the king's house, and
from the roof he saw a woman bathing; and the woman was
very beautiful in appearance.

So David sent and inquired about the woman. And one
said, "Is this not Bathsheba, the daughter of Eliam, the wife
of Uriah the Hittite?" And David sent messengers and took
her, and when she came to him, he lay with her; and when
she had purified herself fom her uncleanness, she returned
to her house. And the woman conceived; and she sent and
told David, and said, "I am pregnant."

Then David sent to Joab, saying, "Send me Uriah the Hittite." So Joab sent Uriah to David. When Uriah came to him,
David asked concerning the welfare of Joab and the people
and the state of the war. Then David said to Uriah, "Go down
to your house, and wash your feet." And Uriah went out of

*2 Samuel 12:10. Taken from *The Living Bible,* Copyright 1971 by Tyndale
House Publishers, Wheaton, Illinois. Used by permission.

the king's house, and a present from the king was sent out after him. But Uriah slept at the door of the king's house with all the servants of his lord, and did not go down to his house.

Now when they told David, saying, "Uriah did not go down to his house," David said to Uriah, "Have you not come from a journey? Why did you not go down to your house?" And Uriah said to David, "The ark and Israel and Judah are staying in temporary shelters, and my lord Joab and the servants of my lord are camping in the open field. Shall I then go to my house to eat and to drink and to lie with my wife? By your life and the life of your soul, I will not do this thing." Then David said to Uriah, "Stay here today also, and tomorrow I will let you go." So Uriah remained in Jerusalem that day and the next.

Now David called him, and he ate and drank before him, and he made him drunk; and in the evening he went out to lie on his bed with his lord's servants, but he did not go down to his house. Now it came about in the morning that David wrote a letter to Joab, and sent it by the hand of Uriah. And he had written in that letter, saying, "Place Uriah in the front line of the fiercest battle and withdraw from him, so that he may be struck down and die." So it was as Joab kept watch on the city, that he put Uriah at the place where he knew there were valiant men. And the men of the city went out and fought against Joab, and some of the people among David's servants fell; and Uriah the Hittite also died . . . .

Now when the wife of Uriah heard that Uriah her husband was dead, she mourned for her husband. When the time of mourning was over, David sent and brought her to his house and she became his wife; then she bore him a son. But the thing that David had done was evil in the sight of the Lord.

The glorious future Abigail saw ahead for David had already been realized for a long time. After David had been king over Judah for seven and a half years, he became the ruler over the entire nation of Israel. During his rule he encountered quite a few storms which affected him and his wives.[1] Despite these difficulties, however, one fact remained the same. He was still faithful toward God. David was a righteous king, treating each of his subjects fairly.

---

1. 1 Samuel 30:1-6

Over and over again the Lord confirmed that He was with David. The name of the God of Israel became highly respected among the nations around Israel.

And then he had taken a walk that fateful evening in the spring. The rainy season which had stopped the war against the Ammonites was over and General Joab and his army had returned to battle.[2] King David, however, did not march with his troops as he used to do. He stayed at home. The idleness was not good for him. One evening when he could not sleep, he got out of bed and walked outside. There, from the roof of his palace, he saw a woman named Bathsheba taking her bath on the flat roof of her house.

David, inactive and shirking his duties as Israel's king, proved to be easy prey for Satan's temptations. He had never, like Job, made a covenant with his eyes not to look with desire on other women.[3] He had never made a deliberate stand against the shameful sin of lust that becomes a destructive fire in the life of the man who commits it.

Peter warned Christians to be watchful against Satan, who like a lion is looking for human prey (1 Peter 5:8). However, God's armor is strong and will stand firm against Satan's attacks (Ephesians 6:11).

Just like that fateful time in paradise—Satan was not very original—temptation again made use of the eyes. Like Eve,[4] David's heart desired what his eyes saw. He did not renounce the desire immediately and radically, and so the evil could no longer be curbed.

Bathsheba was an unusually beautiful woman. Her father, Eliam, was one of David's heroes. Her husband, Uriah, was a dedicated and courageous officer in the king's army who performed his services dutifully and conscientiously.

Was Bathsheba a frivolous woman who was cunningly trying to draw another man's attention now that her husband was away from home? Was she purposely aiming to catch the king—who was sensitive to female beauty—in her nets? Was she seeking to dispel her loneliness? Had her desire to have intercourse with another man become too strong? Or was she only an unsuspecting but negligent

2. 2 Samuel 11:1
3. Job 31:1
4. Genesis 3:6

woman? Did she deliberately omit the necessary precautions to protect herself against improper interests?

There is no reason to begrudge Bathsheba the benefit of the doubt. Maybe the situation was such that she reasonably did not expect to be seen. There is no proof that she had previously seen a man on that section of the palace roof. Was not the king a military man who spent much of his time away from home? The Bible does not say whether she expected the king's invitation or if it took her completely by surprise. It is certain that Eastern monarchs were used to acting this way. But this manner of behavior was unworthy of David, the man after God's heart.

When the call from the royal court arrived, Bathsheba naturally went. As a subject, she had to obey. It remains a secret whether her sexual surrender to the king took place willingly or under protest. The truth remains, however, that she was not the instigator responsible for the dramatic events which were about to develop. But history does give insight into Bathsheba's character, and she was far from being innocent.

Her situation could be compared to that of Joseph's, who courageously said, "How could I do such a wicked thing and sin against God?"[5] She was missing the love, the courage, and the self-control God is willing to give a person,[6] and of which Joseph was an example. The thoughtfulness with which Abigail had earlier approached David when he had been about to forget himself and kill innocent people[7] was painfully absent in Bathsheba. Bathsheba's absence of God-given perception—equal to her sin of adultery—caused her sins.

"David did what was right in the eyes of the Lord, and did not turn aside from anything that He commanded him all the days of his life, except in the matter of Uriah the Hittite."[8]

Bathsheba did not prevent the man after God's heart from forever casting a blame on his own name. Nor did she prevent David from giving Israel's enemies a reason to slander God's name.[9] David insulted God, a thousand years

5. Genesis 39:9
6. 2 Timothy 1:7
7. 1 Samuel 25:23-31
8. 1 Kings 15:5
9. 2 Samuel 12:14

before Christ. Two thousand years after Christ, the flood-lights of Hollywood would still mercilessly reveal the sin of David and Bathsheba.

The Bible doesn't cover anything up. It removes every doubt whether or not David was the father of Bathsheba's child. All the facts gradually came to light, and with those facts appeared the startling development of sin. What started with David's dereliction of duty toward his army developed through deceitful lust—even after he had been told that Bathsheba was married—into murder.

These developments precisely followed the pattern about which James later warned.[10] David's lustful desire lured and enticed him and, because he yielded to it, resulted in death. Literal death came to at least five people.

David's conscience proved to be so dulled that he didn't acknowledge the extent of his deeds until the Prophet Nathan confronted him with them.[11] But by then over nine months had already passed. The man who had experienced a walk with God so intensely that he could sigh, "O God, my God! How I search for You! How I thirst for You in this parched and weary land where there is no water. How I long to find You!"[12] kept silent all those months before his God. And because his perception of God was darkened, he also missed clear sight of himself.

When Nathan placed David's sin before him without mentioning any names, the king pronounced the sentence of death for the delinquent without any hesitation.

It is sad that Bathsheba, the person who could have called David to a standstill, failed to do so. Often in the past David had been open to the advice of other people, whether it came from a woman such as Abigail or from his other subjects.[13] One hint from Bathsheba probably would have been enough to prevent disaster. What Abigail had prevented now happened through Bathsheba. David insulted his God.

The sin of David and Bathsheba started a chain reaction of death and sorrow, for "the thing David had done displeased the Lord."[14] Although according to the law of Moses both deserved to die,[15] God was gracious toward

10. James 1:14-15
11. 2 Samuel 12:1-9
12. Psalm 63:1

13. 2 Samuel 18:3-4
14. 2 Samuel 11:27
15. Leviticus 20:10

them. They would remain alive after David confessed his sin, but their child would die.

There was, furthermore, a double curse on David's life. Because David had dishonored God by taking Uriah's wife, the sword would never depart from his house.[16] He would also be punished for his adultery; another man would publicly dishonor his wives.

These predictions were literally fulfilled. The little baby of David and Bathsheba died right away.[17] Uriah had been killed. Three of David's sons—Ammon,[18] Absalom,[19] and Adonijah[20]—died violent deaths. David's concubines were dishonored by one of his sons in the sight of all Israel.[21]

The Bible not only describes the deeds of men; it also proclaims the greatness of God and His infinite grace. After David realized and confessed that he had, first of all, sinned against God, he was freed from his burden of sin. He became happy because of his rediscovered fellowship with the Lord and expressed life's new meaning in a touching psalm of repentance.[22] His life gained a new dimension which is seen in the jubilant opening lines of another psalm. "What happiness for those whose guilt has been forgiven!" he exclaimed. "What joys when sins are covered over! What relief for those who have confessed their sins and God has cleared their record."[23] David did not excuse himself; he did not minimize what he had done.

Although the Bible makes no mention of Bathsheba's feelings, it seems acceptable to assume that she shared David's sense of guilt and the acceptance of God's forgiveness. Was not the following child God gave to David and Bathsheba their son Solomon, who in due time would be a king known for his wisdom and riches? The Prophet Nathan, whom God had chosen to announce His judgment, called the baby Jedidiah, which meant, "the beloved of Jehovah."[24]

God was gracious to Bathsheba, who later acted as an intermediary through whom her son Solomon became an heir to the throne. The woman who started with a negative role in history became, by God's grace, the wife of Israel's

16. 2 Samuel 12:10
17. 2 Samuel 12:19
18. 2 Samuel 13:28-30
19. 2 Samuel 18:14
20. 1 Kings 2:24-25
21. 2 Samuel 16:22
22. Psalm 51
23. Psalm 32:1-2
24. 2 Samuel 12:24-25

greatest king. She was also the mother of its wisest and richest ruler, Solomon,[25] and appears among the ancestors of the Saviour of the world, Jesus Christ.[26]

The story of David and Bathsheba has become a monument that tells of the faithfulness of God. It stands as an encouragement for every human being who, like David and Bathsheba, has confessed his sin and learned to live by grace.

Yet Bathsheba's story, first and foremost, remains a terrifying, negative example. She was not an inexperienced young girl. She was a married woman who knew how easily the desire of a man could be kindled. She was not a heathen woman ignorant of the laws of the holy God. She was descended from a family where His name had been honored.

Bathsheba did not live within immoral surroundings. Uriah, her husband, had maintained high moral principles. Living a disciplined life, he had subordinated his sexual desires so that he could expend energy toward a higher principle—loyalty to the king. And no doubt Bathsheba knew that the man who had desired her was the king of her people, well-known for his righteous and pious living.

Bathsheba illustrates that a woman needs to maintain a clear perspective on the holiness of God. She must think ahead about the ruinous results of sin and refuse to put a man in a tempting situation. Otherwise she could easily become a curse instead of a blessing.

Bathsheba knew what was right, but she did not do it. That was her greatest sin.[27]

---

25. 1 Kings 1:11-31
26. Matthew 1:6
27. James 4:17

Bathsheba, a woman who did not prevent a God-fearing man from insulting his God
(2 Samuel 11:1-17, 26-27)

Questions:
1. What positive things does the Bible say about David? (Acts 13:22; 2 Samuel 5:10) What negative? (1 Kings 15:5; 2 Samuel 12:10)
2. Do you believe that David was the only person at fault? Why or why not?
3. Could Bathsheba have done anything to prevent David from insulting God? If so, how?
4. List the results of David and Bathsheba's sin. (Read also 2 Samuel 12:1-14.)
5. Study the story of David and Bathsheba in light of James 1:14-15. How did their sin start?
6. What is the greatest warning for you in this story? How can you apply what you have learned?

16

*"Don't be misled; remember that you can't ignore God and get away with it: a man will always reap just the kind of crop he sows! If he sows to please his own wrong desires, he will be planting seeds of evil and he will surely reap a harvest of spiritual decay and death."**

Paul

Jezebel, who forgot that no one can trifle with God

1 Kings 19:1-3 Now Ahab told Jezebel all that Elijah had done, and how he had killed all the prophets with the sword. Then Jezebel sent a messenger to Elijah, saying, "So may the gods do to me and even more, if I do not make your life as the life of one of them by tomorrow about this time." And he was afraid and arose and ran for his life and came to Beersheba, which belongs to Judah, and left his servant there.

1 Kings 21:5-16 But Jezebel his wife came to him and said to him, "How is it that your spirit is so sullen that you are not eating food?" So he said to her, "Because I spoke to Naboth the Jezreelite, and said to him, 'Give me your vineyard for money; or else, if it pleases you, I will give you a vineyard in its place.' But he said, 'I will not give you my vineyard.' " And Jezebel his wife said to him, "Do you now reign over Israel? Arise, eat bread, and let your heart be joyful; I will give you the vineyard of Naboth the Jezreelite." So she wrote letters in Ahab's name and sealed them with his seal, and sent letters to the elders and to the nobles who were living with Naboth

*Galatians 6:7-8. Taken from *The Living Bible,* Copyright 1971 by Tyndale House Publishers, Wheaton, Illinois. Used by permission.

in his city. Now she wrote in the letters, saying, "Proclaim a fast, and seat Naboth at the head of the people; and seat two worthless men before him, and let them testify against him, saying, 'You cursed God and the king.' Then take him out and stone him to death."

So the men of his city, the elders and the nobles who lived in his city, did as Jezebel had sent word to them, just as it was written in the letters which she had sent them. They proclaimed a fast and seated Naboth at the head of the people. Then the two worthless men came in and sat before him; and the worthless men testified against him, even against Naboth, before the people, saying, "Naboth cursed God and the king." So they took him outside the city and stoned him to death with stones. Then they sent word to Jezebel, saying, "Naboth has been stoned, and is dead."

And it came about when Jezebel heard that Naboth had been stoned and was dead, that Jezebel said to Ahab, "Arise, take possession of the vineyard of Naboth, the Jezreelite, which he refused to give you for money; for Naboth is not alive, but dead." And it came about when Ahab heard that Naboth was dead, that Ahab arose to go down to the vineyard of Naboth the Jezreelite, to take possession of it.

(Also read 2 Kings 18.)

Queen Jezebel could hardly contain her anger. As she rested in her summer palace in Jezreel, she listened intently to the report of her husband who had just returned from a trip to Mount Carmel.

"You should have seen what Elijah did," King Ahab said, shaking his head. He then gave his detailed account of what had taken place. He told his wife how Elijah had challenged the priests of the god Baal to measure their strength against the strength of his God. He had, in fact, seen the Lord God at work through the person of Elijah, but he kept that to himself.

In Jezebel's thinking, the God of Israel was equal to Baal. She considered Yahweh to be a local god who carried a message just for the Israelites. Within His supposedly chosen nation, however, Israel's God had been unable to keep pace with that of her god Baal. Therefore the priests of Baal had gladly accepted Elijah's challenge. Were they not in the majority? So 450 priests of Baal were matched against one lone prophet of the true God of Israel.[1]

According to plan, two altars were built. One was for the Lord God, the other for Baal. The true God had to prove Himself by sending fire to light the wood. No human being was allowed to kindle the fire.[2]

The priests of Baal began their ceremonies first, shouting their throats hoarse most of the morning. When they hadn't received a reply by noon—no fire had come down on their altar—they wounded themselves terribly with knives and swords until the blood gushed out. Although they continued to rave all afternoon, their god remained silent. He was a lifeless god, incapable of giving an answer even when 450 of his servants called on him in ecstasy.[3]

Then Elijah started repairing the altar of his God, the living God, which had been torn down. He worked alone, calmly stacking 12 stones, each of which represented one of the 12 tribes of Israel.[4]

To mark the contrast and at the same time to testify to his faith openly, he dug a trench around the altar about three feet wide. Then he arranged the wood and laid an ox on top. Four barrels of water were then poured over the sacrificial carcass and the wood. That ritual was repeated three times, clearly putting Elijah's God at a disadvantage.

After he finished all the preparations, Elijah walked up to the altar and pleaded, "O Lord, answer me! Answer me so these people will know that You are God and that You have brought them back to Yourself."[5]

That very moment fire flashed down from heaven and completely burned up the sacrifice, wood, water, stones, and even the dust. It was a breathtaking and awesome event.

There was no doubt who the true God was. He had proven Himself with great evidence. The Israelite people who had glided away to idolatry came to their senses. Those

1. 1 Kings 18:22
2. 1 Kings 18:23
3. 1 Kings 18:29
4. 1 Kings 18:31
5. 1 Kings 18:37

who had shown no preference at the beginning of the contest were now convinced.

"The Lord is God! The Lord is God!" they shouted.[6] Then fury broke loose against the prophets of Baal. Every one of them was killed next to a nearby brook; not one escaped.

Shortly thereafter, the Lord God answered another prayer of His prophet Elijah. A drought that had harassed the country and its inhabitants for three and a half years came to an end after an announcement by the prophet. Rain that hadn't fallen during those years came down in showers from heaven.

"The water came so suddenly," Ahab said, still obviously frightened, "that even though Elijah told me to leave immediately, I hardly reached the palace before the downpour."[7] When her husband finished his story, Queen Jezebel became livid with rage. She was the daughter of Ethbaal, king of the Sidonians,[8] whose people lived in the country north of Israel. Her father not only was king over his people; he was also a priest of Baal.

After Jezebel married King Ahab, she introduced the worship of Baal into Israel. This religion—crude and inhuman—was known for its child-sacrifices. Because of Jezebel's influence, her husband surpassed everyone else in doing what was wrong in the sight of God. She encouraged him to do every sort of evil.[9] She was firmly dedicated to the worship of idols.

Ahab, a weak man, became a willing instrument in Jezebel's hands and offended the Lord God more than any king before him.[10] The worst of his many sins was his marriage to the idol-loving Jezebel.[11] He, an Israelite king, began serving Baal—because of her and with her.

Through Ahab's influence, Baal then took over the place of the living God in the Israelites' hearts. But Jezebel was not satisfied; she undermined the Hebrew religion till nearly all the people accepted Baal as their god. The queen began to exercise more and more power over her husband, till finally she ruled the people.

6. 1 Kings 18:39
7. 1 Kings 18:44-45
8. 1 Kings 16:31
9. 1 Kings 21:25
10. 1 Kings 16:33
11. 1 Kings 16:30-32

Perhaps Jezebel herself gave the order to kill all the prophets of the God of Israel. But Obadiah, the foreman of Ahab's household, saved the lives of 100 prophets by hiding them in a cave at the risk of his own life.[12]

Jezebel, however, continued to encourage the worship of Baal. She supported the prophets of Baal personally, feeding 400 of them every day at her own table.[13]

After Ahab finished his story, Jezebel was not impressed by the way in which the Lord had dealt with the priests of Baal. She considered His action to be a personal insult.

Naturally her fury unloaded itself on Elijah. In her mind, he was the only person who could be blamed for the recent event. Her words to him were bitter as gall. "You killed my prophets. I swear that I am going to kill you," she stated. "Tomorrow you will be dead."[14]

So mighty was this woman—so evil, so ruthless—that Elijah did not doubt that she would execute her threat. The man who had calmly faced King Ahab and 450 excited prophets of Baal now lost all courage. He fled for his life into the wilderness. "I've had enough," he lamented, crouching under a tree. "Please, Lord, take away my life."[15]

Happily the situation was not nearly as somber as the despondent prophet perceived it to be. There were still 7,000 people who had not bent their knees before Baal and broken their covenants with God.[16] But Elijah only heard about them later.

Jezebel probably thought that she had won a new victory over the living God. Either she did not get the chance to kill Elijah or else she did not use her opportunity because she feared the people's reactions. But her enemy had taken flight and she considered that a victory.

Now no one remained to take the side of God openly. Jezebel had come one step further in her goal to extinguish the worship of Israel's God. Her growing perception of victory made her presumptuous—almost reckless—as she soon demonstrated.

During this time, Ahab began to desire a vineyard which bordered his palace and was owned by a man named

12. 1 Kings 18:4
13. 1 Kings 18:19
14. 1 Kings 19:2
15. 1 Kings 19:4
16. 1 Kings 19:18

Naboth. Wanting to use the piece of land as a royal garden, he offered Naboth a good price for it. Naboth refused, so Ahab offered him a better piece of property in trade. But Naboth again refused the offer. The land was his father's inheritance and Israelite law forbade him to part with it. The property had to remain in the family. Naboth knew that if he parted with it he would be disobedient to the Lord.[17]

Ahab understood Naboth's response, for he knew the Lord's commandments. Yet he sulked about the refusal like a child who didn't get what he wanted and refused to eat. He went to bed, sullenly, and turned his face to the wall.[18]

Jezebel thought her husband's response was utterly stupid. In her homeland no authority ranked higher than the king. "A nice king you are," she railed. "Do you rule this country or not? Get up and eat. Be happy. I'll get you Naboth's vineyard."[19]

Jezebel was an unscrupulous woman who could commit murder without the slightest remorse. Thus she started looking for an acceptable excuse to kill Naboth. After his death, the land could then be claimed by the king. Ironically, she discovered what she sought in the Hebrew religion and used the laws of God that she had always undermined as an excuse to bring charges against Naboth.

Misusing the king's authority, she commanded a call for fasting. This meant that the people would assemble under the assumption of a religious gathering. Fasting in those days meant a humbling of oneself before the holy God[20] who could not leave sin unpunished. In that setting it was easy for Jezebel to set up Naboth as a scapegoat who had released God's wrath. She accused him publicly of having cursed God and the king. Under the laws, anyone who cursed God had to pay the penalty; he had to die.[21]

Jezebel had organized her plans carefully. In order to make the accusation valid,[22] she made sure that two witnesses were present. Even though they were false witnesses, they did exactly what was expected of them.

Thus Naboth, an innocent man, was stoned to death on Jezebel's orders. His sons shared his fate.[23] King Ahab then

17. 1 Kings 21:1-3
18. 1 Kings 21:4
19. 1 Kings 21:7
20. Psalm 35:13
21. Leviticus 24:16
22. Deuteronomy 19:15
23. 2 Kings 9:26

added Naboth's land to his possessions.

Jezebel, who had pretended to take the laws of God seriously, had undermined them once again. The accusation against Naboth had been that he had cursed God and the king. In that way she made the king seem to be as important as God. Again she mocked the living God. Did she think, perhaps, that she had silenced Him forever now that His prophet Elijah still seemed to be out of business?

The moment the king entered Naboth's vineyard to claim it, Elijah suddenly appeared before him. "This is God's message for you," he stated. "Isn't killing Naboth bad enough? Must you rob him too? Because you have done this, dogs shall lick your blood outside the city just as they licked the blood of Naboth[24] and your descendants shall also die similar deaths."[25] Elijah then prophesied about Jezebel, "The dogs of Jezreel shall tear apart the body of Jezebel, your wife, within the boundaries of Jezreel."[26]

The blood of innocent Naboth, his sons, and the prophets of God had not called in vain to God in heaven.[27] Ahab and Jezebel died as predicted.[28]

Jezebel's end, which was particularly terrible, matched her godless rule. Throughout her life, she had continued to be connected with immoral and sorcerous practices.[29] But now God's judgment came swiftly. After being thrown out of a palace window, her body dashed against the ground and was trampled by horses' hooves. Dogs then tore her dead body apart and ate her flesh.

Initially no one noticed Jezebel's corpse. When the decision was later made to bury her—since she had been the daughter and the wife of a king—hardly anything was left of the once proud queen. All the burial party could scrape together were her skull, her feet, and her hands. These body parts were then scattered like manure on a field so that no one could identify them.

God's prophecy about Jezebel had been literally fulfilled. She reaped what she sowed. She sowed on the field of her selfishness and reaped destruction. The words Solomon spoke in the name of God apply to her: "Because I have

24. 1 Kings 21:19   27. 2 Kings 9:26
25. 1 Kings 21:22   28. 1 Kings 22:29-40; 2 Kings 9:30-37
26. 1 Kings 21:23   29. 2 Kings 9:22

called and you refused to listen . . . and you have ignored all My counsel and would have none of My reproof, I also will laugh at your calamity; I will mock when panic strikes you."[30]

God had offered Jezebel many opportunities to turn to Him. As a heathen princess, she had been allowed to live in the land of promise. There she came in contact with His laws and His prophets. She witnessed the great miracles He performed. But she didn't use her opportunities. On the contrary, she mocked the God of Israel and presumptuously committed her evil deeds in the name of religion.

God's love was available to Jezebel, a woman He had created. The many opportunities He gave her to make good use of her life show this. She could have reformed and accepted His grace. God had endowed her with an unusual mind. She was keen, intelligent, and resolute. But she had used those capabilities toward exceptionally bad ends. She had willingly and intensely offered them to the service of evil. She had held a high position and could have had a far-reaching and godly influence. But not only did she do what was wrong in the sight of the Lord herself; she also instigated others to do the same.

Many centuries later, Jesus lamented about the inhabitants of Israel's capital: "O Jerusalem, Jerusalem, killing the prophets and stoning those who are sent to you! How often would I have gathered your children together as a hen gathers her brood under her wings, and you would not!"[31]

Jezebel, likewise, refused to turn to God. She continued to do evil until her death. She proudly believed that she could hold out against God, but that belief turned out to be a painful misconception. No one can trifle with God.

30. Proverbs 1:24-26
31. Matthew 23:37

Jezebel, who forgot that no one can trifle with God
(1 Kings 19:1-3; 21:5-16. Also read 1 Kings 18.)

Questions:
1. Study Jezebel's life carefully and list her character qualities. (Also read 1 Kings 16:31; 21:17-29; 2 Kings 9:30-37.)
2. Compare Jezebel's behavior with the works of the flesh mentioned in Galations 5:19-21. What are your conclusions?
3. Consider Jezebel's life in light of Proverbs 1:20-31 and describe the ways in which you think God reached out to her.
4. What were her responses to Him?
5. What "remarkable" words are said of her husband in 1 Kings 21:25?
6. What lessons did you learn from this story? How will you apply them in your daily life?

17

"Prophecy (Heb. nebu'ah) in the Bible does not concern itself primarily with foretelling future events, in the sense in which one speaks of a weather prophet or a financial forecaster. It deals rather with forthtelling the intuitively felt will of God for a specific situation in the life of an individual or a nation."*

Huldah, a woman who helped lead an apostate nation back to God.

2 Chronicles 34:22-33 So Hilkiah and those whom the king had told went to Huldah the prophetess, the wife of Shallum the son of Tokhath, the son of Hasrah, the keeper of the wardrobe (now she lived in Jerusalem in the Second Quarter); and they spoke to her regarding this.

And she said to them, "Thus says the Lord, the God of Israel, 'Tell the man who sent you to Me,' thus says the Lord, 'Behold, I am bringing evil on this place and on its inhabitants, even all the curses written in the book which they have read in the presence of the king of Judah. Because they have forsaken Me and have burned incense to other gods, that they might provoke Me to anger with all the works of their hands, therefore My wrath will be poured out on this place, and it shall not be quenched.' But to the king of Judah who sent you to inquire of the Lord, thus you will say to him, 'Thus says the Lord God of Israel regarding the words which you have heard, because your heart was tender and you humbled yourself before God, when you heard His words against this place and against its inhabitants, and because you humbled yourself before Me, tore your clothes, and wept

*From *Harper's Bible Dictionary* by Madeleine S. Miller and J. Lane Miller, page 582. Copyright © 1952, 1954, 1955, 1956, 1958, 1959, 1961, 1973 by Harper & Row, Publishers, Inc. Used by permission.

before Me, I truly have heard you,' declares the Lord. 'Behold, I will gather you to your fathers and you shall be gathered to your grave in peace, so your eyes shall not see all the evil which I will bring on this place and on its inhabitants.' " And they brought back word to the king.

Then the king sent and gathered all the elders of Judah and Jerusalem. And the king went up to the house of the Lord and all the men of Judah, the inhabitants of Jerusalem, the priests, the Levites, and all the people, from the greatest to the least; and he read in their hearing all the words of the book of the covenant which was found in the house of the Lord.

Then the king stood in his place and made a covenant before the Lord to walk after the Lord, and to keep His commandments and His testimonies and His statutes with all his heart and with all his soul, to perform the words of the covenant written in this book. Moreover, he made all who were present in Jerusalem and Benjamin to stand with him.

So the inhabitants of Jerusalem did according to the covenant of God, the God of their fathers. And Josiah removed all the abominations from all the lands belonging to the sons of Israel, and made all who were present in Israel to serve the Lord their God. Throughout his lifetime they did not turn from following the Lord God of their fathers.

(Also read 2 Chronicles 34:1-21; 35:1-19.)

Although her name meant "weasel," Huldah fortunately did not allow that to affect her character. Her life did not in any way resemble that shy, marten-like, little animal. During Huldah's time, people were needed who would dare to speak up for their convictions undauntedly, who were not afraid to act.

Huldah was a prophetess, a woman who served as a mouthpiece for God. Her special calling did not place her outside society, for she was a housewife at the same time.

Huldah was the wife of Shallum, the man in charge of King Josiah's wardrobe. Just like every other married woman should, she cared for her husband daily. But her marriage didn't stand in the way of executing her calling. She saw fit to combine one responsibility with the other. Israel at that time also had two male prophets, Jeremiah[1] and Zephaniah,[2] both of whom continually urged the people to return to God.

The Israelite people had left God. They no longer obeyed His Word. The nation had become apostate. Although Israel had turned away from the laws Moses had given centuries earlier, the people were still true to the letter of those laws. According to the laws, the Israelites had been able to count on God's exceptional blessing and prosperity because they were His own exalted people. He had chosen them above all other nations.[3] Those privileges, however, had been tied to one condition; they had to remain faithful to Him.

If they failed to be faithful, the results would be terrifying. If they rejected God, He would reject them.[4] Unforeseen catastrophes would befall them and in the end they would not remain in the land that God through Moses had promised them.[5]

With this call to obedience, God had given His people a measuring stick to live by: His commandments. To enable His people to obey Him, He had carefully described those laws. His people were not left in the dark concerning what He expected from them. They knew exactly what He required.

In order that the Israelites would not forget His commandments, He told them to hide the laws in their hearts. They were to teach their children the Word of God and allow thoughts of Him to permeate their personal lives and those of their families. All their activities were to be influenced by God's leading.[6]

Obeying the Word of God, therefore, would not be too difficult for the Israelites. Obedience to Him did not lie outside their reach or above their strength. On the contrary, they had heard His laws from childhood and carried them in their hearts, ready to recite them at a moment's notice.[7] All God expected from them was their willingness to live ac-

1. Jeremiah 25:3-7
2. Zephaniah 1:1-6
3. Deuteronomy 7:6
4. Hosea 4:6
5. Deuteronomy 28:1-64
6. Deuteronomy 6:6-9
7. Deuteronomy 30:14

cording to His directions. They would do this with His help, through His power. In that way the whole world would be able to see the happiness of a nation that walked with God.

At the beginning, especially as long as the Israelites were led by good kings, everything went smoothly. During the reign of David, who had stayed passionately true to Yahweh, God had blessed Israel. During the reign of David's son Solomon, who had been loved for his piety and wisdom, the fame of Israel spread.

Since that time, however, the Israelites had gradually degenerated spiritually. More and more they had departed from their covenant with God. Few of the previous Israelite kings had turned as far away from God as Manasseh and Amon, the grandfather and father of the present king. Few other kings had been so wicked, so backsliding. None had served the idols so repulsively.[8]

Huldah held court not far from the temple buildings. There, at her post in the new part of Jerusalem, she daily gave the people advice concerning the Lord. In spite of Israel's backslidden condition, there were still a few people who inquired after God.

Huldah carried on her duties openly, without being hindered. She did not need to hide herself as other prophets had been forced to do. For the first time in many years, Judah had a king who served God. King Josiah, following in the steps of his illustrious forefather David, carefully obeyed the laws of God and did not depart from them. Undoubtedly his dedication to God was the result of his mother Jedidah's influence. He began to cleanse the land of idols, tearing down the altars of the false gods and grinding the idols into powder. He also hired workers to repair and improve the temple of God.[9]

In her court, Huldah grew accustomed to the noises of the repairmen. Then, one afternoon, she saw five men approaching her. She easily recognized Hilkiah, the high priest, and Shaphan, the secretary, and several other servants of the king. Their faces were serious, their speech measured.

8. 2 Chronicles 33:1-25
9. 2 Chronicles 34:1-13

"We have special orders from his majesty the king," stated Hilkiah. "It concerns the Law of Moses. I found it in the house of God while we were bringing out the money that we needed for the repair work."[10]

"We have read it to the king," Shaphan continued. "He is frightened because we as a nation have not kept the written Law God has given. His majesty has torn his clothes. He is ashamed about the sin of his people. He understands that the situation is very serious, for he fears the wrath of God."[11]

It was soon clear to Huldah that the men had come to her to discover God's will concerning this newly found book. If she asked herself why the king had consulted her instead of the Prophet Jeremiah, for instance, she didn't show it. Like other prophetesses in the past—Miriam[12] and Deborah[13]—Huldah was used to working with men, calmly and with dignity.

God needed a human being who could speak His Word on earth. Most of the time He used the services of men, but this particular time He used a woman.

Huldah rightly understood that she, as a woman, should not try to compete with men. Neither did she try to escape her responsibilities because she was a woman. God was looking for someone who could function as His instrument; that person's sex was secondary in His plan.

Jehovah be praised, Huldah thought. *Josiah will not treat the Book of the Law like an antiquity and put it away in a collection. He understands that God's Book cannot be treated like an ornament in the royal library. The Law is there to be applied.*

Paul explained this principle clearly when he wrote that it is not the nature of an instrument but its capability that makes it useful for God. It does not matter, for example, whether a vessel is of gold, silver, or earthenware, as long as it is sanctified and "useful to the Master, prepared for every good work" (2 Timothy 2:20-21).

Huldah could not but acknowledge the authority of the just-found Book of the Law. Her answer was clear, without reserve. She showed no respect of persons, for it was God Himself who spoke through her lips, challenging the people.

10. 2 Chronicles 34:14-15   12. Exodus 15:20
11. 2 Chronicles 34:18-19   13. Judges 4:4

"Thus says the Lord, the God of Israel: 'Tell the man who sent you to Me, Thus says the Lord . . . .' " Those four words—"thus says the Lord"—were the words which proved the credibility of her words as a prophetess.[14]

Huldah then predicted the national downfall of the people. They had treated God's Word carelessly and become apostate, serving idols instead of the living God. Hers was a terrible message of doom,[15] but Huldah held nothing back. She was not afraid of the results these words might have for her personally.

Yet God's words did not only contain judgment; they spoke of grace as well. God had noticed the love and faithfulness Josiah was showing toward Him, his sensitive response to Scripture. So He postponed His judgment till after Josiah's death.[16] Then, under King Zedekiah, judgment would be executed over the people. At that time the cup of God's wrath would be full to the brim. Reparation would no longer be possible, because Israel had not responded to God's repeated calls for conversion.[17] The nation had ignored His summons: "O land, land, land, hear the word of the Lord."[18] Jerusalem and the temple would be destroyed and the people forced into exile.[19]

After the messengers delivered Huldah's strong message to the king, there was no doubt in his mind that God had spoken through her. It was also evident to him that immediate action had to be taken.

Right away he went to the temple with the leaders of the people and read the Law of God to all the inhabitants of Jerusalem and Judah, both small and great.[20]

The people listened attentively. Like the king, they were convinced that God had spoken through the Prophetess Huldah. Consequently a revival started among the people which had never been seen before. The king, the leaders, and the entire nation made a new covenant with God. Together they solemnly pledged that from that point on they would serve the Lord. They were willing to obey His Word with all their hearts and souls.

A thorough reformation resulted. The cleansing from

---

14. 2 Chronicles 34:23-24   17. Jeremiah 29:19
15. 2 Chronicles 34:25   18. Jeremiah 22:29
16. 2 Chronicles 34:26-28   19. 2 Chronicles 36:15-21   20. 2 Chronicles 34:30

idols was carefully continued and moral boundaries were set. This cleansing was not restricted to the capital city. The entire country—from northern Geba to southern Beersheba—became involved.[21] Most important of all, the Passover was celebrated again. The Israelites had forgotten how God had delivered them in the past. They had ignored the sacrifice that pointed to the coming Christ. They had forgotten the commemoration of the exodus from Egypt, an event which God through Moses had instituted to be an annual observance.[22] For many years they had not celebrated this feast.

Josiah continued to live up to the norm that God had set for a king. Through Moses, he wrote down the attitude that a king should have toward God's Law: "And it shall be with him, and he shall read in it all the days of his life, that he may learn to fear the Lord his God, by carefully observing all the words of this Law and these statutes."[23]

After Josiah's meditation and application of God's Word, he experienced God's blessing, a truth which many other scrolls had described.[24] As certain as disobedience was followed by God's curse, so obedience was always followed by His blessing.

Listening to the words of Scripture not only changed King Josiah's life; the entire nation changed. It experienced the most thorough reformation of worship Judah had ever known. An apostate nation returned to its living God.

The final judgment of God could not be averted, however. Too many generations of Israelites had sinned too heavily. But the people who lived during the time of the Prophetess Huldah did receive a number of years respite.

Although Huldah's name only briefly lightened up history, the influence of her life was far-reaching. It controlled the destiny of an entire nation because she coupled her name with the Word of God. Huldah knew that Word. Therefore she could freely exhort and encourage other people with it.

Huldah disclosed no secrets of a far future, unlike other prophets and prophetesses. She occupied herself with the

---

21. 2 Kings 23:4-8   23. Deuteronomy 17:18-19
22. Exodus 12:1-17; 23:14-15   24. Joshua 1:8; Psalm 1:1-3

task of revealing God's will through a medium that He had used for centuries. She applied His will to the special situation of the Israelite nation and its individual people. She helped them rediscover lost truths. When her people once again gave their attention to the Word of God—listening to it, reading it, studying it, meditating on it—marvelous things began to happen. When human beings are willing to do what God expects of them, things happen that no one had ever thought possible.

Huldah, like many other women, was a housewife. But her commitment to the Word of God and her courage to ally herself strongly with it distinguished her from most of her countrymen. When the great opportunity in her life arose, she was prepared.

Huldah, a woman who helped lead an apostate nation back to God
(2 Chronicles 34:22-23; also read 2 Chronicles 34:1-21; 35:1-19.)

Questions:
1. What was Huldah's two-fold task?
2. Why was Huldah chosen to announce judgment? What proved that she spoke in the name of God?
3. What instructions had God given to the Israelite king? (Deuteronomy 17:18-19)
4. What did God expect from His people concerning His Law? (Deuteronomy 6:6-9; 30:14)
5. What changes took place after Huldah had spoken?
6. What effect does God's Word have in your life? Are there possible changes you want to make after observing Huldah's life?

New Testament

18

*"When she [a woman] chooses to do good, she blesses more than ever a man can. But the moment she surrenders to sin, her hatred toward the men of God is much more passionate, much fiercer, much more fatal. She will stop at nothing then."**

Abraham Kuyper

Herodias, a woman who degraded herself through revenge and murder

Mark 6:17-28 For Herod himself had sent and had John arrested and bound in prison on account of Herodias, the wife of his brother Philip, because he had married her. For John had been saying to Herod, "It is not lawful for you to have your brother's wife." And Herodias had a grudge against him and wanted to kill him; and could not do so; for Herod was afraid of John, knowing that he was a righteous and holy man, and kept him safe. And when he heard him, he was very perplexed; but he used to enjoy listening to him.

And a strategic day came when Herod on his birthday gave a banquet for his lords and military commanders and the leading men of Galilee; and when the daughter of Herodias herself came in and danced, she pleased Herod and his dinner guests; and the king said to the girl, "Ask me for whatever you want and I will give it to you." And he swore to her, "Whatever you ask of me, I will give it to you; up to half of my kingdom." And she went out and said to her mother, "What shall I ask for?" And she said, "The head of John the Baptist." And immediately she came in haste before the king and asked, saying, "I want you to give me right away the

---

*From *Women of the Old Testament* by Abraham Kuyper, page 60. Copyright © 1933, 1961 by Zondervan Publishing House. Used by permission.

head of John the Baptist on a platter." And although the king was very sorry, yet because of his oaths and because of his dinner guests, he was unwilling to refuse her. And immediately the king sent an executioner and commanded him to bring back his head. And he went and beheaded him in the prison, and brought his head on a platter, and gave it to the girl; and the girl gave it to her mother.

"The head of John the Baptist," hissed Herodias.[1] There rang no hesitation in her voice, no trace of doubt. Around her many other people were talking. A select group of people had gathered together in the palace to celebrate the birthday of King Herod Antipas. Many eminent leaders, high military officers, and prominent guests from Galilee had come to the banquet at the ruler's invitation.[2]

Salome, Herodias' daughter, bent cautiously over to her mother and asked, "What shall I ask for?"[3]

With that question, Herodias could hardly suppress a triumphant smile. Revenge flashed in her eyes. She was not at a loss for an answer, not even for a second. She claimed the head of the prophet, John the Baptist.

Herodias' plan had succeeded. Today she would finally rid herself of the man she hated more intensely than anybody else. Where words had failed, slyness had succeeded. Herod, her husband, would now be forced to kill John. Hadn't he just told Salome in the presence of everyone, "Ask me for anything you like and I will give it to you"? He had even confirmed those words with: "Even half my kingdom!"[4]

Herodias knew her husband's inclination toward cruelty. He shared that family streak with his father, Herod the Great.[5] Herod was not a man of high morals. After all, hadn't he repudiated his lawful wife—an Arabian princess—for her, Herodias, the wife of his brother Philip? Hadn't both of them deserted their original life-partners in order to live together?

Herodias also was well aware of her husband's pride and sensuality. These traits formed the basis of her speculation

1. Mark 6:24
2. Mark 6:21   4. Mark 6:23
3. Mark 6:24   5. Matthew 2:13

and the reason that she had challenged Salome a few moments earlier to dance before the guests. In this time and surroundings, such dancing was a usual thing to do at a feast, though not for the orthodox Jews.

The lascivious dance of the girl excited those present; her movements fascinated the people who had spent the evening eating and drinking. Deciding that this voluntary—and in his eyes fantastic—achievement had to be rewarded highly, the king made his unjustifiable statement.

Herodias also knew that Herod was not a courageous man. He would not dare to acknowledge that he had impulsively promised something he, in fact, didn't really want to deliver. He would not admit that the life of a fellowman did not belong to the kingdom of an earthly ruler. Although the disposal of a life was not in his hands, in this situation he would not concede that his oath was invalid and of no power.

Proud and egotistical, Herod would choose for his own interests and against those of the prophet. But Herodias had to force that decision on him. Her husband hesitated to harm John of his own accord.

This was not the first time that Herodias had tried to kill John the Baptist. Up to this point her husband had always protected the prophet from her schemes. Every attempt she had made to take John's life had failed. But now she finally had set up a cool and calculating snare for Herod. She had done it so cunningly that her husband unexpectedly was caught in it. The game for the head of John the Baptist was over. Herodias had won.

Her gruesome deed had not sprung from a sudden impulse. She had not acted in an excess of insanity. She had worked on this devilish plan for almost a year and a half. These facts form the background of the ghastly drama that was about to unfold.

The way Herod and Herodias openly lived together mocked the laws of the people among whom they were living. The laws of God condemned what they were doing in very clear words. "If a man takes his brother's wife, it is impurity; he has uncovered his brother's nakedness, they shall be childless."[6]

It was difficult, however, for the subjects of Herod and Herodias to rebuke them. The monarch and his spouse were people of high authority. They represented the Roman emperor whose troops occupied the Jewish country.

But then a man had come who was not deterred by their royal authority. He spoke in the name of God. He, John the Baptist, carried out his orders without respect of persons. His message was strong and simple: "Repent, for the kingdom of heaven is at hand."[7]

His voice, in which the roughness and harshness of the desert where he had lived[8] could still be heard, resounded throughout the Jewish land.

The message was not unknown. Earlier prophets, men like Moses[9] and Jeremiah,[10] had extended the same call to conversion. They, too, had exhorted the nation to improve its way of living. If the Israelites would have repented, God would have forgiven their sins and restored their land.[11]

John's preaching, however, was extremely urgent; the kingdom of heaven was at hand. "Prepare a road for the Lord," he stated. "Straighten out the path where He will walk."[12]

Many people recognized the voice of God. They flocked to John in great numbers and confessed their sins. As proof of their changed hearts, they were baptized.

John's voice did not only knock at the doors of his fellow citizens. It also sounded on the gates of the palace of the tetrarch, Herod's proper title.[13] The title of "king," though flattering, was incorrect since he only ruled over the provinces of Galilee and Perea, a quarter of the Jewish land.

Herod and Herodias were not Israelites but Edomites, descendants of Esau. Jacob, from whom the Israelites descended, was not their forefather. They did, however, share the patriarchs Abraham and Isaac with the Israelites. They were distantly related to the Jews among whom they were living.

The message of the prophet was not intended for the

6. Leviticus 20:21
7. Matthew 3:1-6
8. Luke 1:80

9. Deuteronomy 30:9-11
10. Jeremiah 18:11
11. 2 Chronicles 7:14

12. Matthew 3:3
13. Luke 3:19

Jewish nation alone. It was also intended for Herod and Herodias, for they, too, had to repent. They needed to turn back from the wrong direction in which they were heading. God had a message for them. After their conversion, forgiveness and repair would be available to them.

John was not satisfied to leave them with a general warning. He did not hesitate to warn the couple personally. "It is not right that you have your brother's wife," he told Herod frankly.[14] He also pointed to other crimes that Herod was committing.[15]

A greater difference between the righteous, resolute prophet and the immoral, wavering Herod would hardly be thinkable. Yet a certain relationship had developed between the two men. The king was attracted to the prophet in spite of the fact that John always told Herod the hard truth. He recognized characteristics in John that he was missing himself: uprightness and a holy way of living. So Herod had summoned John many times in order to listen to him speak. As a result the king became increasingly confused, but no spiritual changes occurred in his life.

Herodias experienced the yielding of her husband to the prophet as an additional threat. The woman through whose influence two marriages had been derailed wanted to be sure she was not repudiated. From the moment that John had exposed their sinful relationship, she had hated him—the disturber of her peace. She would get him, somehow!

Herodias wanted to prevent Herod, most of all, from getting further under the influence of the Baptist. So she asked that John be imprisoned and finally it was done. The possibility of killing him now seemed to be within her reach, for the prison was accommodated within the walls of the fort housing the royal family.

Herod continued to be watchful, however, for his own sake as well as John's. He knew that John's death could result in an uproar, for the people unquestionably considered him to be a prophet.[16] His shaky "throne" might not be able to outlive such an upheaval.

Thus the prophet who started to bring the people back to

14. Mark 6:18
15. Luke 3:19-20
16. Matthew 14:5

God was locked up in prison. The man of whom Jesus said, "Among those born of women there has risen no one greater than John the Baptist,"[17] was taken captive. He was the prey of a mean, bloodthirsty woman and a cruel, wavering man. Bereft of his freedom, he sat chained—day after day, week after week—till he finally doubted his own calling.[18]

Herodias proved her hatred. With deathly precision she set her snares around John. She also trapped Herod in those snares by undermining his watchfulness.

Like many parents, Herodias had the characteristic of using her child for her own advantage. Even her own daughter was sacrificed to her devilish scheming, of which the final phase now had arrived.

Salome, influenced by her mother, did not waste any time bringing her request before the king. Her reactions were even more heartless than her mother's. Salome realized that her horrible mission required haste. Her work had to be done quickly, before the mood of the king changed. Otherwise he might take back his reckless offer.

"Give me the head of John the Baptist immediately," she stated cruelly. "And I want it to be presented on a plate."[19]

Even Salome's mother hadn't gone that far. But the hatred of the mother had poisoned the thoughts of the daughter. For Salome, it was not enough that John would be murdered without an open trial, interrogation, or any type of defense. She was not satisfied that he had to leave this life without saying farewell to his friends. John would continue to be deeply humiliated after his death; the plate with his stiffened head supplied the dessert of Herod's birthday party on the explicit requests of Herodias and Salome.

High festive days were opportunities during which monarchs often showed grace, but Herodias horribly degraded this festive day. She murdered an innocent man whose only "crime" had been that he spoke the words of God fearlessly, and made two of her relatives accomplices in her crime.

17. Matthew 11:11
18. Matthew 11:2-6
19 Mark 6:25

Although the names Herod and Herodias meant "heroic," seldom have the meanings of names been such a flagrant contradiction to the life of their bearers. Their deed did not sprout from heroism. On the contrary, they were dictated by hell.

The portrait gallery of the Bible shows many sinful women, but few of them were as wicked as Herodias. Not many had their hands as stained with blood as she did. The possibility to repent was clearly offered to her, but she rejected it, thus committing her greatest sin.

Before John had been taken to prison, he had pointed out a man who traveled in the Jewish land, preaching and doing many miracles—Jesus of Nazareth. "Look! There is the Lamb of God who takes away the sin of the world," the Baptist had said.[20] And he added, "I am not of any importance, He is.[21] I am only His herald, the voice who announces Him, the finger who points to Him."

The Jews understood this symbolism. Those words foretold that Jesus—like an innocent lamb under their covenant with God[22]—would give His life to redeem them. From now on no more animal sacrifices would be needed to substitute for sinful man. Jesus was the announced Messiah—the Saviour of man, of His people, of the entire world.[23]

John exhorted Herod and Herodias so that they might also have a part in this new relationship with God. But to do so, they had to be willing to be humbled. They had to confess their sins, to renew their lives. John wanted them to meet the Messiah who was already living among them. But the couple refused to answer God's call.

Jesus, the Son of God, identified with sinful men enough to take their death sentence on Himself. In that way God's requirement that the sinner had to die was met; His judgment was on Christ instead of on mankind. The guilty goes free because the Innocent took the penalty (Isaiah 53:5-12). Whenever a person admits and confesses his sin and receives Christ as Saviour, he receives pardon and forgiveness from God. Salvation is now accessible to everyone.

How differently the Samaritan woman responded in a similar situation. Like Herodias, she was publically known for her immorality.[24] She also was visited personally,

20. John 1:29
21. Mark 1:7
22. Exodus 12:1-16
23. John 3:16
24. John 4:18

though by Jesus Himself[25] rather than John.

That woman, realizing that sin had brought her to a blind alley, came to a saving belief. Her life radically changed and became a blessing to others. Other people in her village came to a faith in Jesus Christ through her witness.[26]

With Herodias, however, the opposite had happened. Her life degenerated. She became a curse to her environment. She had the cruelty to burden the conscience of her own child with the blood of one of God's chosen servants. Her daughter Salome never showed signs of repentance. Her conscience, like her mother's, was seared beyond recovery.

Herodias also had a destructive influence on her husband. Initially, God had seen an opening with Herod for conversion. The door of his heart had stood ajar for faith till, through Herodias' influence, that door had slammed shut.

When Jesus some time later was sentenced to death, He paid attention to Pilate. At His cross, He even opened heaven for a murderer.[27] But He had nothing to say to Herod.[28] Herod had lost his opportunity. Like Herodias, he had not listened when God spoke to him through John. Both experienced the fact that God often speaks to a person more than once.[29] But when people don't heed His calling, they may lose their chance forever.

Herod, who once had tried to prevent the death of John the Baptist, took an actual part in Jesus' death.[30] He continued the murderous tradition of his family. His heart had been hardened.

Herodias' life would have been different if she had corrected herself in time and listened to God's warning. Unfortunately, Herodias preferred sin; she ignored the love of God, who had warned her in time. By refusing to accept the solution to her problem, she invited disaster on herself. She hardened her heart[31] against the teachings of God. Herodias' greatest sin was not adultery or murder; it was unbelief.

"Whoever loves discipline loves knowledge, but he who hates reproof is stupid."[32] Those are the words of Solomon, the wisest man of all time.

25. John 4:7-26
26. John 4:28-39
27. Luke 23:39-43

28. Luke 23:9
29. Job 33:14
30. Luke 23:8-12

31. Proverbs 28:14
32. Proverbs 12:1

"Keep hold of instruction, do not let her go," he also cautioned. "Guard her, for she is your life."[33] "He who rejects reproof goes astray."[34]

Herodias rejected the reproof that was meant for her good, and the consequences were disastrous, both materially and spiritually.

Flavius Josephus wrote that Herodias' ambition became her downfall. She overestimated her influence on Herod and incited him to ask Emperor Caligula for the king's title. The request was refused, Herod was exiled, and for the rest of his life he was despised.* Herodias shared her husband's humiliation. Such was the reward of a woman who, because of revenge, degraded herself to commit murder.

Herodias, a woman who degraded herself through revenge and murder
(Mark 6:17-28)

Questions:
1. Why did Herodias want John the Baptist killed? What means did she use to accomplish that goal?
2. How did Herodias' evil influence affect her husband and daughter?
3. How could John the Baptist's warning have influenced Herodias' life?
4. What sins did Herodias commit? Which do you consider to be the worst? Why?
5. Study Deuteronomy 30:9-10 and 2 Chronicles 7:14. What are the requirements for God's blessing?
6. Are there times in your own life when you fail to listen to God's directions and so miss part of His blessings?

---

*Flavius Josephus, *Antiquities of the Jews,* Book XVIII, Chapter 7.

33. Proverbs 4:13
34. Proverbs 10:17

19

*"Salome was ambitious for her sons, and ambition is commendable when it is in full agreement with the mind and purpose of God. Ambition, when divinely directed, can lead to the heights of honor but when selfishly pursued can cast one down to the depths of degradation."**

Herbert Lockyer

Salome,
a mother who thought to ask
the best for her children

Matthew 20:17-28 And as Jesus was about to go up to Jerusalem, He took the twelve disciples aside by themselves, and on the way He said to them, "Behold, we are going up to Jerusalem; and the Son of Man will be delivered up to the chief priests and scribes, and they will condemn Him to death, and will deliver Him up to the Gentiles to mock and scourge and crucify Him, and on the third day He will be raised up."

Then the mother of the sons of Zebedee came to Him with her sons, bowing down, and making a request of Him. And He said to her, "What do you wish?" She said to Him, "Command that in Your kingdom these two sons of mine may sit, one on Your right and one on Your left."

But Jesus answered and said, "You do not know what you are asking for. Are you able to drink the cup that I am about to drink?" They said to Him, "We are able." He said to them, "My cup you shall drink; but to sit on My right and on My left, this is not Mine to give, but it is for those for whom it has been prepared by My Father." And hearing this, the ten became indignant at the two brothers.

*From *The Women of The Bible* by Herbert Lockyer, page 151. Copyright © 1967 by Zondervan Publishing House. Used by permission.

But Jesus called them to Himself, and said, "You know that the rulers of the Gentiles lord it over them, and their great men exercise authority over them. It is not so among you, but whoever wishes to become great among you shall be your servant, and whoever wishes to be first among you shall be your slave; just as the Son of Man did not come to be served, but to serve, and to give His life a ransom for many."

Salome, the mother of John and James,[1] resolutely took a few steps forward. Her sons followed her. She did not care that she would interrupt Jesus. She did not wait till He had finished talking. Salome had something on her heart to ask the Master—something that could not wait.

It was nearly Passover and Jesus and His disciples were once again making the trip from Galilee to Judea. An increasing number of people had flocked together around them to go up to Jerusalem to celebrate the Feast of Passover. Among them were the sick, the lame, and the blind—people who wanted Jesus to heal them.

The long journey through the countryside and across the Jordan River finally was finished. Then the group reached Jericho. The final miles which still separated them from Jerusalem could not be underestimated. The heaviest part of the trip—the climb over the steep and barren Judean hills—still lay ahead of them.

On the surface there did not seem to be much difference between this journey and the previous ones. But the disciples of Jesus knew better. The shadows of the Master's future suffering were darkening His life and disturbing Salome's thoughts and those of His other friends.

The words which Jesus had spoken just before the small group left Galilee came to mind over and over again.

"I am going to be betrayed into the power of those who will kill Me," He had said.[2] That statement had caused them sorrow since they now understood that He soon would part from them.

Only a few moments ago, He had again repeated those words and elaborated on them. Leaving the crowds alone

1. Matthew 27:56; Mark 15:40
2. Matthew 17:22-23

for a brief while, He pulled His disciples aside.

"As you see," He said to them, "we are on our way to Jerusalem. The Son of Man is to be delivered into the hands of men, and they will kill Him, and He will be raised on the third day."[3]

These were astounding words. They revealed that Jesus, who came for His own people, would be rejected by them.[4] Although the religious leaders of the Jews would sentence Him to death, their decision would not cool down their hatred for Him. Before He died, they would mock Him, humiliate Him, and try to make a fool out of Him. The Man who had done only good would be openly executed like a common criminal.

Immediately preceding this terrible event, Jesus desired His fellow travelers to share His anguish. Were not His best friends among them—Peter, John, and James—as well as Salome and the other women who had so faithfully served Him? Few people were closer to Him and knew Him any better. They would share His feelings, His sorrow.

Salome was the first and only person to respond to Jesus' words. Her voice sounded serious, but what she was saying had nothing to do with the Master. Her words had no real connection to His statements. Mother Salome showed no compassion toward the Saviour and His approaching sufferings. She thought only of herself and her boys.

When John the Baptist started preaching over three years earlier, the sons of Zebedee initially had joined him. Later, when Jesus walked along the Lake of Galilee and called them, they had left their work and immediately followed Him.[5]

My sons may have an impetuous nature, and sometimes show insensitivity of character, Salome thought, *but they are, in fact, spiritual men. I understand why the other disciples have given them the surname "sons of thunder,"[6] yet their hearts are open toward the things of God.*

That was the reason why she and her husband, Zebedee, had not kept John and James from their intention to follow the Master. They had let their sons go without grumbling,

3. Matthew 20:18-19   5. Mark 1:19-20
4. John 1:11   6. Luke 9:54-55

without asking preference for their own interests.

Zebedee had a prosperous fishing business, and his own sons could hardly be spared. They formed the hub around which much of the work centered. When the sons left, the business became much more dependent on the other workers and that was not advantageous.

Yet, as parents, they had given this sacrifice gladly. They were happy that James and John—whom they had given God-fearing educations—had reacted so positively. Deep in their hearts they were grateful that their sons were interested in God and were not eager to become rich.

It was a privilege for James and John—and their parents, indirectly—to be chosen as disciples of the Nazarene. The parents' gratitude had increased when they saw that John, who had a special place in Jesus' heart, gradually became His best friend.

These thoughts must have been in Salome's mind. For that reason she began to worry. After Jesus' repeated announcement of His suffering, the troubles that would result began to fill Salome's thinking.

What will happen to my boys when the Master is gone? Salome asked herself. *They have built their hopes on Him. Their futures are dependent on Him.*

In her thoughts Salome repeated Jesus' words. Then she realized that He had not only spoken of dying; He had also mentioned the resurrection.

That's it! Salome thought, relieved. *Jesus' final destination is not death. He will rise from the dead and set up His kingdom. Soon He will rule over His people as king.* These and similar thoughts which occupied the disciples and many other people[7] were also in her mind.

Now she knew what she had to do. Right away, she had to make sure that the future of her sons was assured. And who could better speak up for children than their mother?

For that matter, did not she herself have rights? Hadn't she sacrificially given of her life to the Master? Hadn't she shared the inconvenience of wandering about the countryside? Hadn't she given Him of her time and possessions?

---

7. John 6:15; Acts 1:6

And, as the sister of Jesus' mother,[8] couldn't she claim a special privilege?

She quickly took a few steps forward. Then she knelt down before the Master to show her respect.

"What can I do for you?" Jesus asked kindly.[9]

Without further introduction, she uttered her request. Her words gave vent to her train of thought. "Promise that my two sons may be sitting next to You in Your kingdom," she begged, "one at Your right hand, the other at Your left."[10]

Salome said what she had intended to say. Didn't it strike her that these words would sound harsh and egotistical in the Master's ears? Didn't she realize that He painfully experienced the absence of her love? Did she, even in part, sense how poorly she had responded to the situation of this moment? Was she aware how small-minded her request was standing next to the greatness of the suffering that awaited the Master? The innocent Son of God was about to die and the only things Salome could think about were the futures of her sons.

While the Son of God as a man stood staring in the face of death, longing for understanding and compassion, Salome only harbored feelings of motherly pride.

It is not clear whether Salome spoke for herself or if she was also the mouthpiece of her sons.[11] But even if the latter were true, it did not place her in a better light. It did not decrease her responsibility. On the contrary, her question revealed that she had missed the opportunity to correct them.

Because of Salome, the Lord now was not only suffering through the ambition of a mother. He was also suffering because He was being deserted by her sons—two of His best friends.

His other friends didn't come through any better. A short while later all the other disciples became furious over the requests of John and James. They did not react angrily because they knew that this request of the two fellow disciples had been painful to Jesus. On the contrary, they felt

8. Mark 15:40-41; John 19:25   10. Matthew 20:21
9. Matthew 20:21   11. Mark 10:35-45

insulted for themselves—passed by. Now it was utterly clear how important James and John thought they were. Who were they to consider themselves so much more prominent than the rest?

Salome's words were heartless toward Christ, but they also showed little feeling for the mothers of His other disciples.

Why, the other women might well have been asking themselves, *should the sons of Zebedee be privileged again? Isn't it time that others—our sons—should be coming to the front? Haven't Peter and Andrew and the other disciples left all as well? Haven't they also followed the Master?*[12]

In spite of Salome's motherly pride, Jesus didn't rebuke her. The Son of Man standing before her was also God, able to probe into the deepest corners of a human heart. He not only recognized her selfish and negative traits, but saw more. He discerned her thoughts and desires. Her entire inner being lay open and bare before Him. He read her heart like a book.

No doubt it was frightening, but it was also encouraging. No one but the Creator of a mother's heart knows how her heart—with every fiber of its being—is attached to the child to whom she has given birth. He understood how vulnerable mothers are in this world, even in their relationships to God. He realized how easily a small child can come between its mother and Himself. He saw the daily struggle mothers have gone through in this regard. Christian mothers were not exempt from such feelings.

So the Master didn't reprimand Salome. He understood and forgave. He knew that, next to her shortcomings, Salome had faith. She believed in His future, even though her view was humanly shortsighted and thus wrong. Jesus tasted her love through her desire to ensure that her sons would always stay close to Him.

Jesus valued Salome's loyalty. She had served Him faithfully from the beginning and continued to do so even after the warrant for His arrest had been issued in Jerusalem.

12. Matthew 19:27

For this reason, Jesus didn't deny Salome her request. Instead, He corrected it. Although at that moment she didn't recognize it, the answer to her prayer would come in an entirely different way than she had expected.

Salome didn't know what she was asking. Thinking along human standards, she considered honor and reputation to be exceptionally great favors. Jesus, however, was led by godly thinking. The greatest honor in heaven was reserved for people who suffered because of their faith.

So His understanding response, addressed to John and James, went right over Salome's head. "Are you able to drink from the terrible cup I am about to drink from?"[13]

The Lord Jesus was about to establish a heavenly kingdom instead of an earthly kingdom. The seats of honor in that kingdom would be allocated by God—His Father—and not by Him. The gate to that kingdom hinged upon suffering, the suffering of the Son of God.

How bitter His suffering was; every drop from His cup of suffering was mixed with gall. Salome experienced Jesus' suffering a few days later when she stood at the foot of His cross. Accompanied by His mother and several other women, she experienced parts of that suffering with Him. She was there when He shouted in agony of spirit: "My God, My God, why have You forsaken Me?"[14]

This heart cry was directed to His Father in heaven, who at the beginning of Jesus' earthly ministry had said to Him: "You are My only Son, the Man after My heart."[15]

Paul, in the letter to the Philippians, explains how we may understand these two seemingly contradictory statements. He wrote that Jesus "emptied Himself, taking the form of a bond servant, and being made in the likeness of men. And being found in appearance as a man, He humbled Himself by becoming obedient to the point of death, even death on a cross" (Philippians 2:6-8). Because of Jesus' willingness to serve and die for mankind, God highly exalted Him and gave Him a name which is above every name. At the name of Jesus, everyone on earth, in heaven, or under the earth will bow and confess that He is Lord (Philippians 2:9-11).

The Lord's kingdom was founded on suffering and obedience. Salome's sons would get a place in that kingdom. But they had to enter it in the same way in which

13. Matthew 20:22
14. Matthew 27:46
15. Mark 1:11

the Master would. He, the pioneer of salvation, would suffer heavily in order to bring many sons to glory.[16] He would hand out suffering as a favor, as a privilege, as a grace.

The most sparkling crown a person can wear is not forged by respect and honor, but by unconditional obedience. The Bible states that the Son of God learned obedience in the school of suffering.[17] For His servants, there is no other way. Their measure of suffering—if undergone in the name of Christ—destines their future joy in glory.[18]

James and John already had an ample part in that suffering. But happily their pain was still hidden from their mother. Salome requested exceptional privileges for her sons and received them, expressed in suffering rather than a show of honor and glory.

The painful experience of suffering is not something a person chooses naturally. No human being likes suffering; he cannot. In light of eternity, however, the suffering of a Christian is easier to bear when he looks at the school of suffering taught by Christ and at the glory of eternal life with God (2 Corinthians 4:17-18). Through reliance on God's promises in the Bible, Christians who are willing to reap the fruits of suffering also grow to understand its hidden blessings. "For to you," Paul wrote to the Christians at Philippi, "it has been granted for Christ's sake, not only to believe in Him, but also to suffer for His sake" (Philippians 1:29).

Was Salome still alive when her son James, the first of the apostles to be martyred, was killed by the next king, Herod Agrippa I?[19] She never knew that her other son, John, was exiled at the end of his life for the sake of the Gospel.[20]

James and John would not dominate the surroundings of an earthly king. But later, in heaven, they would radiate with a martyr's crown because of the sufferings they went through in the name of Christ.

How much of her suffering Salome understood is not known.

At the cross, Salome was treated exceptionally well. Jesus appointed her son, John, to take care of His own mother.[21] The Saviour granted to the disciple whom He loved above the others the honor to serve. Serving, like suffering, is a pillar on which the everlasting kingdom of God is being constructed. In this way, the principles of the kingdom of God are diametrically

---

16. Hebrews 2:10
17. Hebrews 5:8
18. 1 Peter 4:12-13
19. Acts 12:1-2
20. Revelation 1:9
21. John 19:25-27

opposed to those of earthly rulers.

Jesus brought this lesson to the attention of the women and His disciples that day at Jericho. His disciples should desire to impress through service rather than through domination. The people who are willing to be the least on earth will be counted the highest in heaven.

It is valuable for every mother to consider Salome's request for her sons carefully, especially those mothers who—though they are aware of their human shortcomings and limitations—love the Lord deeply and are seeking the best for their children. They can learn many principles from this passage, especially in the area of prayer. Mothers must learn not to be too hasty in their prayers for their children. They must pray unselfishly and thoughtfully.

But there is also great encouragement connected with the story of Salome. God knows what is really best for a child and He wants to provide it, even when the mother asks for the wrong thing.

Salome, a mother who thought to ask the best for her children
(Matthew 20:17-28)

Questions:
1. Formulate Salome's request to Jesus in your own words.
2. What motives do you believe induced her to make this request?
3. How was her request answered?
4. Which characteristics and experiences are given the highest value in the kingdom of God?
5. Briefly study the box on suffering by reading the two references listed in the box. What strikes you?
6. Did you, through this story, gain new insight into the Word of God? If so, what did you learn and how can it be applied to your life?

*" 'Woman Lies Dead In Her Home For Ten Months'
Mrs. B. was found dead in her home in The Hague.
A pile of mail in the hallway allowed the police
to determine that the woman died ten months ago.
There was no crime connected with it."**

Mary Magdalene, a woman who led the way in following Christ

John 20:1-18 Now on the first day of the week Mary Magdalene came early to the tomb, while it was still dark, and saw the stone already taken away from the tomb. And so she ran and came to Simon Peter, and to the other disciple whom Jesus loved, and said to them, "They have taken away the Lord out of the tomb, and we do not know where they have laid Him."

Peter therefore went forth, and the other disciple, and they were going to the tomb. And the two were running together; and the other disciple ran ahead faster than Peter, and came to the tomb first; and stooping and looking in, he saw the linen wrappings lying there; but he did not go in. Simon Peter therefore also came, following him, and entered the tomb; and he beheld the linen wrappings lying there, and the face-cloth, which had been on His head, not lying with the linen wrappings, but rolled up in a place by itself.

Then entered in therefore the other disciple also, who had first come to the tomb, and he saw, and believed. For as yet they did not understand the Scripture, that He must rise again from the dead. So the disciples went away again to

*Taken from *Trouw,* July 24, 1974, page 2. Published by *Trouw*/Kwartet B.V., Amsterdam, The Netherlands.

their own homes. But Mary was standing outside the tomb weeping; and so, as she wept, she stooped and looked into the tomb; and she beheld two angels in white sitting, one at the head, and one at the feet, where the body of Jesus had been lying. And they said to her, "Woman, why are you weeping?" She said to them, "Because they have taken away my Lord, and I do not know where they have laid Him."

When she had said this, she turned around, and beheld Jesus standing there, and did not know that it was Jesus. Jesus said to her, "Woman, why are you weeping? Whom are you seeking?"

Supposing Him to be the gardener, she said to Him, "Sir, if you have carried Him away, tell me where you have laid Him, and I will take Him away."

Jesus said to her, "Mary!"

She turned and said to Him in Hebrew, "Rabboni," (which means, Teacher).

Jesus said to her, "Stop clinging to Me; for I have not yet ascended to the Father; but go to My brethren, and say to them, 'I ascend to My Father and your Father, and My God and your God.'"

Mary Magdalene came, announcing to the disciples, "I have seen the Lord," and that He had said these things to her.

Mark 16:9 Now after He had risen early on the first day of the week, He first appeared to Mary Magdalene, from whom He had cast out seven demons.

Magdala was situated at the northwestern shore of the Lake of Galilee, about three miles from the well-known city of Capernaum. There Mary met Jesus for the first time. There He delivered her from Satan, who through his demons had taken possession of her. There the miracle of her life had taken place, a miracle the full extent of which she could only understand gradually.

Until that meeting Mary of Magdala had been a pitiable woman. She only understood how much she was to be pitied when she saw other possessed people. They could no longer fit into normal society. Almost more animal than human, they roved about in caves—lunatic men and women with distorted faces and wild eyes. Created by God, they were strangled by Satan.

After Jesus commanded the seven demons to leave Mary, everything about her changed. Her bound spirit became free; her cramped limbs relaxed. The glance of her eyes became as calm as the surface of the nearby lake on a quiet day.

Mary would never be able to express exactly what had happened to her. The experience was too great to tell. Only one person understood it completely: Jesus. So she refused to leave Him after her healing. She left Magdala—a thriving place of industry—and went with Him.

Mary Magdalene wanted to stay close to Jesus for many reasons. First, she knew by experience that she could not afford to minimize the power of Satan. Unless she stayed close to the Lord—who was superior to the devil—she alone would have no defense against Satan's attacks. She had to prevent the evil one from possessing her again. If that should happen, her end would be worse than before.[1]

Although Mary stayed close to Christ to protect herself, it was not her only reason. She also followed Him out of love and gratitude. She wanted to do more than just give Him her possessions and calmly stay at home telling the people of Magdala what had happened to her.

Mary Magdalene, who once was possessed by the devil, now had received another passion. Jesus Christ had taken hold of her. He had turned her from darkness to light, from the power of Satan to God[2]—literally.

That change would affect her entire future life. From now on, Mary would acknowledge only one Lord. She chose to follow Him, whatever the cost, till the end. Thus she had accompanied Jesus and His disciples, as had other women who had also been healed of demonic possession.[3]

Early that resurrection morning, the streets were quiet. The sun was not up yet. Darkness enveloped the narrow streets of Jerusalem, but Mary Magdalene hardly noticed. Neither was she aware of the other women around her: Salome,

1. Luke 11:24-26
2. Acts 26:18
3. Luke 8:1-3

Joanna, Mary the mother of James and Joseph, and some others.[4] Yet, as a group, they were on their way to the grave of Jesus to finish embalming His body. They had stopped their work Friday night because the Sabbath observance had begun.[5]

They walked rapidly toward the Place of the Skull, located just outside the city, and made good progress. The merchants who in a few hours would make the narrow streets even narrower with their displays of goods had not yet arrived. The beggars who would ask for alms with outstretched hands and starry eyes were still asleep.

Mary Magdalene walked in front of the little group. She was not interested in what was happening around her. Her thoughts ran only one way. They departed and arrived at the same point: the Master.

Over and again, her thoughts flashed back to the events of the past days. During the trip from Galilee to Jerusalem, the disciples and the other women who were with Jesus had felt heavy-hearted; Jesus had told them what would be awaiting Him.

In spite of His prediction, their entry into Jerusalem had been festive. Great crowds had enthusiastically met them, out of themselves for joy. "Hosanna to the Son of David," they had shouted. "God bless the Man who is coming in the name of the Lord! Hosanna to God in heaven."[6] While uttering these shouts of joy, many had taken off their coats and spread them on the road before Jesus. Others cut branches from the palm trees and did the same with them.[7]

The ecstasy did not last long. A few days later the same inhabitants of Jerusalem cried, "Away with Him! Crucify Him!"[8]

The suffering Mary Magdalene's Master had endured from that point on knew many phases. But Mary had followed Him faithfully till the end had come.

She had been present in the judgment building when the crowds demanded His life. She heard Governor Pilate submitting Him to the fury of His enemies. Her heart had shrunk when she saw how the people mocked and scourged

4. Luke 24:10
5. John 19:31   7. Matthew 21:8
6. Matthew 21:9   8. John 19:14-16

her Master, who had shown so much love to them.

She followed Him when He carried His cross down the street from Pilate's residence toward Calvary, the place where the pronounced judgment was executed. The street that Jesus may have walked is now called the Via Dolorosa, which means, "The Road of Sorrows."

Greatly concerned, Mary watched how the scourging wore the Master out, how He stumbled under the weight of the cross. Like many other people in Jerusalem, she shed tears because of the Master's pain, because of her own sorrow. She had been powerless to do anything for the One who had done everything for her.

At the cross, Mary Magdalene and the other women saw the nails driven through His hands and feet. They watched as the soldier drove a spear into His side, and blood and water dripped onto the ground.[9] At that moment her eyes had searched in vain for the disciples. All of them except one—John—had deserted their Master.

Terrible events which were hard to understand had followed quickly, one after the other. At midday the sky suddenly turned dark and remained that way for three hours. A strong earthquake broke rocks and opened graves. Many godly men and women who had died came back to life again.[10]

Of all the terrible events that happened, the most impressive to her was Jesus' cry shortly before His death: "My God, My God, why have You forsaken Me?"[11]

Why, she had asked herself with painful thought, *did Jesus have to be so forsaken by God and men? Why couldn't He save Himself? Wasn't He powerful? Didn't He have more power than Satan and death?*

Repeatedly Mary Magdalene had watched Jesus' power over disease, infirmity, and demon possession. Even nature had obeyed His voice. A gusty wind had changed into a peaceful breeze and whitecaps had become a sea of rippling glass.

Why, cried a voice within her, *didn't He use His power to help Himself? Why? Why not?*

9. John 19:34
10. Matthew 27:45-53
11. Mark 15:34

Though Jesus' suffering was hard to behold, Mary of Magdala stayed till everything was over and Jesus had spoken the words "It is finished."[12] She could not loosen herself from the Master who had meant more to her than anybody else.

She was present at His burial and afterwards, when everyone had gone home—except Mary the mother of James and Joseph—she placed herself near the grave. She didn't leave the gravesite till Jewish law ordered her to do so when the Sabbath began.

But now the Sabbath was over, and while the whole city slept the women neared the grave. They were relieved; after a day of forced rest they could finally do something. Thinking about their approaching destination, the problems connected with Jesus' body came to their minds. "How can we ever roll the stone away from the entrance of the cave?" they asked one another.[13] And that was not their only problem. Pilate had stationed a guard at the grave and had sealed the stone entrance to keep Jesus' disciples from stealing the body.

About the time the women arrived, the sun had risen. There was no one else around. Jesus' mother and His disciples had not made an early morning visit to the grave.

From a distance they looked at the huge stone. Then they held their breath. Were their eyes deceiving them? No, there could be no doubt; the grave lay open. The stone had been rolled away.

Mary Magdalene turned around right away instead of looking into the tomb. Jesus' disciples had to know of this turn of events immediately. As quickly as she could she hurried to the house of Peter and John. "They have taken the Lord's body out of the tomb," she declared breathlessly, "and I don't know where they have put Him."[14]

Peter and John returned with Mary. Unlike the women, they did not stay outside the rock-hewn cavern. They stepped inside and discovered—by the orderly way the graveclothes were lying—that Jesus' body had not been stolen. Dazed and unsure, the disciples returned to the city.

12. John 19:30
13. Mark 16:1-4
14. John 20:2

Mary, however, could not leave the last spot where the body of her Lord had been placed. She remained outside the tomb, tears flowing freely down her cheeks.

Impulsively, she bent over to look into the tomb one last time and looked straight into the eyes of angels. Wearing shining white robes, two men were sitting at the place where Jesus' body had lain—one at the head, the other at the feet. "Woman, why are you crying?" they asked her.[15]

"Because they have taken away my Lord, and I don't know where they have put Him," she replied, wiping away her tears with her hand.[16] Then, as if her eyes were still searching for Him, she turned away from the tomb and saw someone else standing outside. *It is the gardener or Joseph of Arimathea,* she thought.

"Woman, why are you crying?" the Man asked her.[17]

Mary was looking for one person only, her Master. It didn't occur to her that the gardener would not know her thoughts. Without any introduction, she said, "Sir, if you have taken Him away, tell me where you have put Him, and I will go and get Him."[18]

Mary Magdalene had been faithful to her Lord since her conversion. She had stayed at the cross till the last moment and had been the first at His tomb. Now she wanted to complete her last act of love toward the Master by anointing His body with embalming oil.

Then she heard His voice: "Mary!"[19]

Only one person ever pronounced her name in that way. Nobody else was able to give it the same depth, that radiating warmth. A stream of feelings welled up within her; bewilderment, joy, gratitude, and adoration strove for the preference.

"Rabboni," was all Mary could utter.[20] It was the intimate word for Master in the homely Aramaic, the language Jesus had used when He talked with her.

At that moment Mary Magdalene became the first witness of Jesus' resurrection. The central truth on which the salvation story hinges was first revealed to her. What a privilege!

---

15. John 20:13
16. John 20:13
17. John 20:15

18. John 20:15
19. John 20:16
20. John 20:16

The words Jesus spoke proved that, though He was alive again, from that point on things would be different. He prevented her inclination to hold His feet. "Don't touch Me, for I haven't yet ascended to My Father," He said. "But go find My brothers and tell them that I ascend to My Father and your Father, My God and your God."[21]

With that commission, the risen Lord also made Mary the first announcer of His resurrection. That honor was not reserved for John, His intimate friend, or Peter, His most prominent disciple. Even Jesus' mother did not enjoy this privilege. It was reserved for Mary of Magdala, the woman who led the way in following Christ.

The story of Mary Magdalene is so remarkable that it is described by all four evangelists. In the enumeration with other women, her name is always mentioned first—except at the cross. There Jesus' mother naturally came first.[22] The name of Mary of Magdala, however, occurs no less than 14 times in the Gospels. Each of the evangelists also writes that Jesus was first seen by Mary Magdalene after His resurrection.

Unfortunately Mary Magdalene's name is sometimes connected with immorality. People speak of her as if she were an immoral woman, a prostitute. Perhaps that trend of thought is derived from the Jewish Talmud, which states that Magdala—known for its dye-works and primitive textile factories—had an immoral reputation and was destroyed because of its sexual misbehavior.

In 1324 in Naples, Italy, a home for fallen women was named the Mary Magdalene House and has unfortunately added to the confusion.

Some people identify her with the sinful woman about whom Luke wrote shortly before he mentioned the name of Mary Magdalene.[23] But it is only speculation.

The weak spot that Satan used to make inroads into Mary's life is not known. But it is clear that the Bible speaks only about her earlier demon possession and not of any immorality.

Before Mary met Jesus, her life had been a drab night-

21. John 20:17
22. John 19:25
23. Luke 7:37-50

mare. After He liberated her from the power of Satan, she began to live a meaningful life. This new life through Christ received an added dimension on the morning of Jesus' resurrection. The earthly relationship with her Master was finished but a new, spiritual one began. Seven weeks later, on the Day of Pentecost, the Holy Spirit was given to the believers.[24] Although her name is not mentioned, Mary was certainly among the people present.[25]

The Day of Pentecost gave Mary the answer to her question why Jesus couldn't have saved Himself from death. He not only was the Lord; He was also the Christ, the Saviour, according to Peter's magisterial address. Later Peter described Christ's death more extensively: "Christ also suffered. He died once for the sins of all of us guilty sinners, though He Himself was innocent of any sin at any time, that He might bring us safely home to God. But though His body died, His spirit lived on."[26]

God forsook His Son at the cross because He loved men and wanted everyone who believed on Jesus Christ to have everlasting life instead of everlasting death.[27]

Christ ascended to heaven, but His Holy Spirit descended to convince the people of God's thoughts concerning sin, righteousness, and judgment, and to lead people into God's truth.[28]

The very same Holy Spirit also helped Mary to continue to remain close to Christ. He gave her the power to witness of Him.[29] She also experienced what Paul later would write: "He died for all so that all who live—having received eternal life from Him—might live no longer for themselves, to please themselves, but to spend their lives pleasing Christ who died and rose again for them."[30]

Since the time of Mary Magdalene, millions of women have lived and most of their names have been forgotten. But Mary's continues to live on.

When archaeologists laid bare the former foundations of Magdala nearly 2,000 years later, that name reminded them of Mary Magdalene and the news reached the international press. For centuries poets and painters have been inspired

24. Acts 2:1-21
25. Acts 1:14
26. 1 Peter 3:18

27. John 3:16
28. John 16:8-11
29. Acts 1:8

30. 2 Corinthians 5:15

by her. For example, she influenced the Flemish master Peter Paul Rubens in his renowned painting "Descent of the Cross."

The story of Mary first of all sheds light on Jesus Christ. It shows His love for a person and His power over Satan. But it also clearly shows the attention He gave to a woman. Her story illustrates the fact that God does indeed reserve exceptional privileges for women when they give themselves out of love and gratitude totally to Him.

Mary Magdalene, who led the way in following Christ. (John 20:1-18; Mark 16:9)

Questions:
1. Describe the situation of Mary Magdalene before she met Jesus Christ (Luke 8:2).
2. Study Mark 5:1-13 and 9:17-27. How did demon-possessed people behave?
3. What dangers does a person face who has been healed from demon possession? (Luke 11:24-26) Which spirit should therefore occupy the heart of a person? (1 Corinthians 6:19-20)
4. How did Mary Magdalene's attitude change after she met Christ?
5. What exceptional privileges did Mary receive?
6. List some of Mary Magdalene's godly characteristics. What area of your life needs to be cleansed by God's power?

*"There has never been, in the long history
of the church, such an exhibition of Christian
stewardship and a sense of individual
responsibility in the sight of God."**
Herbert Lockyer

Sapphira,
for whom listening to Satan
resulted in death

Acts 4:32—5:11 And the congregation of those who believed
were of one heart and soul; and not one of them claimed that
anything belonging to him was his own; but all things were
common property to them. And with great power the
apostles were giving witness to the resurrection of the Lord
Jesus, and abundant grace was upon them all. For there was
not a needy person among them, for all who were owners of
lands or houses would sell them and bring the proceeds of
the sales, and lay them at the apostles' feet; and they would
be distributed to each, as any had need. And Joseph, a
Levite of Cyprian birth, who was also called Barnabas by the
apostles (which translated means, Son of Encouragement),
and who owned a tract of land, sold it and brought the
money and laid it at the apostles' feet.

But a certain man named Ananias, with his wife
Sapphira, sold a piece of property, and kept back some of
the price for himself, with his wife's full knowledge, and
bringing a portion of it, he laid it at the apostles' feet. But
Peter said, "Ananias, why has Satan filled your heart to lie to
the Holy Spirit, and to keep back some of the price of the

*From *The Women of the Bible* by Herbert Lockyer, page 153. Copyright © 1967
by Zondervan Publishing House. Used by permission.

land? While it remained unsold, did it not remain your own? And after it was sold, was it not under your control? Why is it that you have conceived this deed in your heart? You have not lied to men, but to God."

And as he heard these words, Ananias fell down and breathed his last; and great fear came upon all who heard of it. And the young men arose and covered him up, and after carrying him out, they buried him.

Now there elapsed an interval of about three hours, and his wife came in, not knowing what had happened. And Peter responded to her, "Tell me whether you sold the land for such and such a price?" And she said, "Yes, that was the price." Then Peter said to her, "Why is it that you have agreed together to put the Spirit of the Lord to the test? Behold, the feet of those who have buried your husband are at the door, and they shall carry you out as well."

And she fell immediately at his feet, and breathed her last; and the young men came in and found her dead, and they carried her out and buried her beside her husband. And great fear came upon the whole church, and upon all who heard of these things.

Who had the idea first, Ananias or Sapphira?

Which one decided to sell a piece of property in order to give the money away to needy people?

It was a marvelous plan, unselfish and sacrificing.

Captivated by a movement that had recently arisen in Jerusalem, Ananias and Sapphira joined a group of people whose dearest desire was to make other people happy. Later these people would be called Christians,[1] named after their Saviour and great example, Jesus Christ.

In Jerusalem, something special had happened. Ten days after the ascension of Jesus, the Holy Spirit had descended on His followers exactly as predicted. That Spirit had captivated the hearts of the believers, changing them radically. A mutual bond of love and unity grew among them such as no one had ever thought possible. They experienced a relationship that had never before existed and which afterwards was largely forgotten.

1. Acts 11:26

The believers met daily with one another in the temple. They wanted to be together. They sought out one another and ate their meals together. God was central in their thoughts and conversations.

In such situations, social differences can be painful. How can one enjoy his possessions when other people have deep needs? The Spirit of Jesus—about whom the apostles told emphatically—had come to live within them. It was His compassion that they experienced. Like Him, they wanted to serve others, to make other people happy. From that point on they wanted to be good stewards of their possessions. Without anyone urging them to do so, the rich sold their possessions. The proceeds were then placed in a mutual fund from which everyone received his share as he needed it.

The first church of Jesus Christ was inwardly united through faith in Him. Its members were also equal in their outward circumstances, because the privileged members gave of their possessions in favor of the needy.

Joseph, also called Barnabas, was a particularly striking man among them. His name meant "Son of Encouragement," and that is exactly what he was. He sold the field he owned and brought the money to the apostles. Everyone began to talk about this man and the good example he had set.

Since the church was thinking spiritually, its members were convinced of the relative and temporal value of earthly possessions. Had not the Master said with much emphasis that unless a person renounced all he had, he could not be His disciple?[2]

Since their thoughts were first of all concerned with the things of the kingdom of God, the Christians were convinced that God would take care of them.[3] Hadn't Jesus assured those who would give up relatives, homes, or property for Him and the Gospel that they would receive back 100 times over?[4]

No wonder that the believers who were living according to these godly standards were popular with all of the people.

2. Luke 14:33
3. Matthew 6:33
4. Mark 10:29-30

Every day people who believed in Jesus Christ, the resurrected One, were added to the church.[5]

In those days, many mighty miracles were happening which filled everyone with awe, including Ananias and Sapphira. Under no other pressure than that of their own consciences, this couple decided voluntarily to follow the examples they saw around them. They didn't want to fall behind Barnabas and the others. Their splendid decision to sell a piece of land and give the earnings away was mutual.

Satan had viewed the developments of the first Christians with hatred. He was looking for ways to curtail their growth and happiness. Because every person who joined the church was a loss for his kingdom,[6] he could not remain inactive.

Satan looked into the hearts of Ananias and Sapphira and discovered that their faith was not of the same quality as that of Barnabas. He discovered that they had a double motive. They wanted to do good, on the one hand, and sought to make an impression on the other.

Ananias and Sapphira were not only concerned about the poor. They also desired to gain honor and admiration for themselves. Their aim was in part unspiritual. They wanted to show themselves better than they were. Maybe fear had also crept in after their initial decision. Now that they were older, they were less cared for and the future was uncertain.

Whatever their reasons, they agreed to keep part of the money from the property they had sold for themselves, while pretending that they gave it all. Otherwise people would not think as highly of them as they did of Barnabas. Fully aware of their well-thought-through decision, Ananias and Sapphira carried out their plan at the cost of their lives.

When Peter accepted the money from Ananias, he knew that deceit was being practiced. His terrifying greeting was: "Ananias, why has Satan filled your heart to lie to the Holy Spirit and to keep back part of the proceeds of the land?"[7]

Peter's words disclosed the extent and the seriousness of the deception. Ananias had allowed Satan to occupy his heart. Like the first couple on earth, Adam and Eve, he and Sapphira had surrendered themselves to be deceived by

5. Acts 2:43-47
6. Acts 26:18
7. Acts 5:3

Satan.[8] As always, Satan was aiming to destroy the work of God.

Peter knew that deceiving the Holy Spirit was deceiving God. "The property was yours to sell or not, as you wished. And after selling it, it was yours to decide how much to give," Peter continued. "How could you do a thing like this? You weren't lying to us, but to God!"[9]

With those words Ananias dropped dead. He was not condemned because his gift was not large enough, but because it was connected with dishonesty. His good deed came to nothing because of his double-heartedness and ly-ing. He had, first of all, failed God, and then tried to dupe the needy. His decision put God's holiness in the balance, and dishonored Him through deceit. That cost him his life.

The God whom Ananias and Sapphira had largely ig-nored is a holy God. He is a consuming fire.[10] No creature is hidden before Him, but all are open and laid bare to His eyes.[11] This was also true of the thoughts of Ananias and Sapphira. They, too, had to give account of their deeds to God, and who could exist when He administered justice in-stead of mercy?

Petrified, the people who were present watched as the younger men covered Ananias' body with a sheet and im-mediately carried him away to be buried.

Jerusalem was small. From any point in the city, it was a short walk to the temple square. When her husband still had not returned home after about three hours, Sapphira went out to investigate. When she entered the room to speak with Peter and the apostles, they were still thinking about the terrible thing which had happened. In the distance sounded the footsteps of the young men returning from Ananias' burial.

Did Sapphira sense the tension filling the room?

Is that the reason that she didn't dare to ask where her husband was?

Nobody told her what had happened. She would also have to stand the test her husband had taken and failed.

Peter took up the thread of conversation with Sapphira as

8. Genesis 3:1-8   10. Hebrews 12:29
9. Acts 5:4   11. Hebrews 4:13

if no time had passed since the death of Ananias. "Tell me, did you sell the land for such and such an amount?"[12]

God was giving Sapphira a second opportunity. She had missed the first one—the chance to respond with her husband in an honest way toward God and His followers.

"A person is a slave to whatever controls him," Peter has written (2 Peter 2:19). Christians must not rationalize even the smallest habit if they know that it is contrary to the Holy Spirit's leading and outside the true freedom that Christ has given to them through His death and resurrection.

Sapphira had not been a good helper for Ananias.[13] She had not used the great influence she had as his wife to bless her husband. She had done him little good. She had not tried to prevent sin, and therefore she was also guilty of his death.

Sapphira also showed herself to be in the power of Satan. So her answer was forcibly short and without hesitation. "Yes, for so much."[14]

"How could you and your husband even think of doing a thing like this, conspiring together to test the Spirit of God?" Peter lashed out at her.[15]

The terrifying fact of the sin of Ananias and Sapphira was that it was premeditated. They were fully aware of what they were doing. Sin had not taken them by surprise; they played with it deliberately. For her sin, Sapphira also died.

Meanwhile the young men returned to the house. They were just in time to bury Sapphira.

Sapphira made an impression, indeed. But it was not a positive one. She left behind memories of fear, fright, and dismay with both the Christians and all those outside the church who heard about the cause of her death.

Sapphira's name meant "sapphire," but the only sparkle she was able to give was that of a grim warning.

---

12. Acts 5:8   14. Acts 5:8
13. Proverbs 31:12   15. Acts 5:9

Sapphira, for whom listening to Satan resulted in death
(Acts 4:32—5:11)

Questions:
1. List some characteristics of the Christian church at the time of Sapphira.
2. What do you believe was the most striking attribute of the believers?
3. How did the attitude of these Christians influence the lives of Ananias and Sapphira?
4. Examine Sapphira's attitude toward her husband in light of Proverbs 31:12. What is your conclusion?
5. How did Sapphira's death affect the Christians?
6 What principle did you learn from this story that you can apply to your own life?

*"I pray Heaven to bestow The Best of Blessings
on This House and on all that shall hereafter
inhabit it. May none but honest and wise
men ever rule under this roof."**
John Adams

Mary of Jerusalem, whose home functioned as the house of God

Acts 12:1-17 Now about that time Herod the king laid hands on some who belonged to the church, in order to mistreat them. And he had James the brother of John put to death with a sword. And when he saw that it pleased the Jews, he proceeded to arrest Peter also. Now it was during the days of the Feast of Unleavened Bread.

And when he had seized him, he put him in prison, delivering him to four squads of soldiers to guard him, intending after the Passover to bring him out before the people. So Peter was kept in the prison, but prayer for him was being made fervently by the church to God. And on the very night when Herod was about to bring him forward, Peter was sleeping between two soldiers, bound with two chains; and guards in front of the door were watching over the prison.

And behold, an angel of the Lord suddenly appeared, and a light shone in the cell; and he struck Peter's side and roused him, saying, "Get up quickly." And his chains fell off his hands. And the angel said to him, "Gird yourself and put on your sandals." And he did so. And he said to him, "Wrap your cloak around you and follow me."

*The second president of the United States. Taken from the mantlepiece in the reception hall of the American Ambassador's Residency in The Hague.

And he went out and continued to follow, and he did not know that what was being done by the angel was real, but thought he was seeing a vision. And when they had passed the first and second guard, they came to the iron gate that leads into the city, which opened for them by itself; and they went out and went along one street; and immediately the angel departed from him.

And when Peter came to himself, he said, "Now I know for sure that the Lord has sent forth His angel and rescued me from the hand of Herod and from all that the Jewish people were expecting." And when he realized this, he went to the house of Mary, the mother of John who was also called Mark, where many were gathered together and were praying.

And when he knocked at the door of the gate, a servant-girl named Rhoda came to answer. And when she recognized Peter's voice, because of her joy she did not open the gate, but ran in and announced that Peter was standing in front of the gate. And they said to her, "You are out of your mind!" But she kept insisting that it was so. And they kept saying, "It is his angel." But Peter continued knocking; and when they had opened, they saw him and were amazed. But motioning to them with his hand to be silent, he described to them how the Lord had led him out of the prison. And he said, "Report these things to James and the brethren." And he departed and went to another place.

The night had long since fallen over Jerusalem. The houses of Israel's capital city were completely dark, for the oil lamps had been put out some hours ago.

Yet, in the house of Mary, all the lamps burned brightly. But no one could see light from the outside, so carefully had the windows been covered. Not even a small ray of light peeped out. People on the street were kept from knowing what was going on inside the home.

Were the people in the house doing something so bad that it could not stand to be exposed to the light? Not at all.

The people in Mary's house were Christians, followers of Jesus Christ. They had been meeting together in this house for some time. They had left the adjoining room of the temple—their old meeting place—because it had become too dangerous. Now Mary's home out of necessity functioned as a church.

These Christians formed a minority group. Such a heavy persecution of believers had broken out that many had fled outside Jerusalem.[1] Those who stayed behind were constantly in danger. The threat of arrest and prison hung over their heads as the sword of Damocles. They were grateful that Mary, a prosperous widow, had placed her home at their disposal.

"My house is spacious enough," she said. "Why don't we have the meetings at my place? My home can easily function as a church building."

Mary didn't seem worried about her own life. Because she loved God, she accepted matter-of-factly that the coming and going of many people meant work, expense, and inconvenience.

Thus Mary of Jerusalem revealed herself as a courageous and sacrificial woman. In some ways she resembled Martha and Mary, who during a time when Jewish leaders were trying to kill Jesus[2] were not afraid to meet Him. She was an indispensable link in the chain of life in the early church.

Mary missed the support of her husband. Was she therefore more drawn toward God? Was she aware of the fact that in the past He had proven Himself strong toward widows who trusted Him?

Wasn't the Prophet Elijah kept alive during famine by a widow?[3] Wasn't the Prophetess Anna—the first woman privileged to see the Child Jesus in the temple[4] and one who heralded His entrance into Jerusalem—also a widow?

The reason that Christians were together this night and hadn't gone home at the usual time stemmed from an emergency. They were in great trouble. Peter had been arrested by King Herod Agrippa.

The Jewish leaders, jealous because of the signs and miracles the apostles were performing, had put believers in

1. Acts 8:2
2. John 11:54-54; 12:1-11
3. 1 Kings 17:7-16
4. Luke 2:25-38

prison before.[5] And though God Himself, by means of an angel, had delivered His servants from prison, the opposition remained. Stephen's blood had been shed,[6] and the people desired more.

No good could be expected from Herod. The hatred against Jesus and His followers permeated the family of this ruler. Hadn't his grandfather, Herod the Great, forever entered history as the man who murdered the children in Bethlehem?[7] And hadn't his predecessor, Herod Antipas, beheaded John the Baptist?[8] Herod Agrippa himself had recently killed James, the brother of John and a disciple of Jesus.[9]

There was no doubt that Peter would also die, probably in public. Then everybody would see what the king thought about the followers of Jesus and his treatment of them.

The believers gathered together to pray on the night which seemed to be the last one of Peter's earthly life.

Peter, meanwhile, was sound asleep, despite being locked up in the prison with chains on his hands. He was not lying awake from fear, wondering what might happen to him the next day. The 16 soldiers who guarded him in groups of four were not keeping him from his sleep.

Yet no human being would be able to deliver him. He was completely locked away from the outside world. An impassable wall stood between him and freedom. The guards guaranteed that he could not break out. "But earnest prayer for him was made to God."[10] Although the way out might be totally closed, the way up remained open.

With strong, preventive use of force, Herod Agrippa wanted to make sure that Peter was not liberated by his friends. But those friends, though having no might of themselves, through prayer had a weapon against which King Herod had no power.

Hadn't Christ given many promises in connection with prayer before His ascension? "I also tell you this, if two of you agree down here on earth concerning anything you ask for, My Father in heaven will do it for you."[11] He had also promised that "where two or three gather together because

5. Acts 5:17-20
6. Acts 7:57-60
7. Matthew 2:16
8. Matthew 14:1-12
9. Acts 12:2
10. Acts 12:5
11. Matthew 18:19

they are Mine, I will be right there among them."[12]

"You can get anything—*anything* you ask for in prayer," Jesus had said, "if you believe."[13]

Another time Christ illustrated His challenge not to slow down in prayer with the example of a widow who had continued to ask and eventually received what she asked for.[14]

The disciples knew that these promises hadn't lost their power. They were still valid, even though Jesus was no longer on earth with them. They knew that He supported their prayers in heaven, that He was interceding for them,[15] and that He would answer them.

The Christians who met in Mary's house believed that the prayers of righteous people had great power and would have wonderful results.[16] Thus it happened that while they were, after the words of the Prophet Isaiah, leaving God no rest,[17] He answered. A supernatural messenger, an angel, decended into Peter's prison. The darkness of the night vanished when he arrived. Iron chains broke, and dropped to the ground.

After the angel had released Peter's chains, he led him outside, unhindered by closed doors. He made the guards deaf and blind and they did not notice what was happening. Peter, aroused from his sleep, experienced what was happening like a dream. In a few moments he stood outside, not knowing whether he was awake or asleep.

While the believers naturally were ignorant of what was happening, Peter was on his way to Mary's house. After a moment of consultation with himself, he realized that he was not dreaming. Thankful to God for his freedom, he headed straight for the home of Mary.

The believers experienced the truth of what God had said centuries ago through the mouth of Isaiah: "I will answer them before they even call to Me. While they are still talking to Me about their needs, I will go ahead and answer their prayers."[18]

After the Holy Spirit came down on the Day of Pentecost, many Christians sold their houses or properties and offered the proceeds to other needy believers.

12. Matthew 18:20
13. Matthew 21:22
14. Luke 18:1-8
15. Hebrews 7:25
16. James 5:16
17. Isaiah 62:7
18. Isaiah 65:24

Mary had not done that. She did not sell her spacious home and give away the proceeds. Instead, she kept her house but placed it at the disposal of the church.

Mary was an independent woman led by God in an individual way. She realized that there were different ways to serve God. She could serve God and her fellowman with the money she received from selling her possessions. But she could also serve God—as He had led her—by sharing the possession itself with those in need.

God has provided the church with apostles, teachers, and prophets (1 Corinthians 12:28). But others are also needed to take their place in the Body of Christ. Every member of Christ's church has a functional gift or possession and is expected to exercise it accordingly (Romans 12:4-7). God in His wisdom has given each Christian his own specific gift, so that every member may rejoice in his uniqueness and be willing to share that gift with others (1 Corinthians 14:12).

Mary understood that the gifts the Holy Spirit distributed among Christians differed. The church of Christ was like a mosaic, for it contained many forms and many colors.

Mary continued the tradition of the women who had lived close to Christ, supporting Him with their private means.[19] She occupied her own place in the mosaic of the church. Her task was as important as those of people who in the eyes of the public seemed to be more prominent. Her influence in the church was undeniable, irreplaceable. God made Peter's travels to preach the Gospel and his opportunity to work miracles again[20] partially dependent on people like Mary of Jerusalem. Mary had her function within the church. But that was not all of her responsibility; she also was the mother of John Mark.[21]

As a mother, Mary experienced the joy of knowing that her son was serving the Lord. Her life not only influenced outsiders; it also affected her own son.

Did God reward the mother through the opportunities He was giving to the son?

John Mark received the exceptional privilege of becoming the helper of Paul and Barnabas.[22] Later he became the traveling companion of Peter, who lovingly called him "my son."[23]

19. Luke 8:3
20. Acts 3:6-8; 5:15
21. Acts 12:12
22. Acts 12:25; 13:5
23. 1 Peter 5:13

What the fellowship with these three great men in the kingdom of God meant for Mark and how it influenced his character can easily be imagined.

The Bible mentions Mary's name only once, and the emphasis is not on her but on her home. According to a legend, this is the same home in whose upper room Jesus celebrated the last supper with His disciples.

According to tradition, John Mark—the writer of the Gospel of Mark—traveled to Alexandria after Barnabas' death. There he founded a church and served as its first bishop till he died or was martyred around A.D. 62. His remains may have been stolen from Alexandria by Venetian soldiers around A.D. 815 and placed under the Church of St. Mark in Venice.

The rest of Mary's life is veiled. But one day, God's Book of Remembrance—the book in which He records the deeds of men and women[24]—will be opened. Only then will it become clear what Mary has meant to the Kingdom of God.

Until that time she will continue to be a stimulus to every woman, widow or not. She showed what a tremendous influence a godly woman can have who puts her home at the disposal of God.

Mary of Jerusalem, whose house functioned as the house of God
(Acts 12:1-17)

Questions:
1. In which way did Mary follow the examples of other women who served Christ? (Luke 8:3)
2. List and summarize the contributions of other women in the Bible who placed their homes at the disposal of God. (See 1 Kings 17:10-22; 2 Kings 4:8-11.)
3. Describe the purpose for which Mary's house was used. What were the results of her hospitality?
4. What do you think Mary's attitude was toward her possessions?

5. Share how you would have felt when Peter came to your door for shelter during a time of persecution of Christians. In your opinion, which of Mary's characteristics gave her the strength to risk possible imprisonment or even death?
6. In light of Matthew 18:19-20, how might your home be used to further the kingdom of God?

*"In country after country some of the most attractive
people I meet are single missionaries. They are absolutely the most life-affirming people anywhere. They
obviously channel their creative drive and
energies to help others around them in Jesus'
name. I watch them and I'm inspired."**

Ada Lum

Phoebe,
a single woman who possessed the
antidote to loneliness

Romans 16:1-2 I commend to you our sister Phoebe, who is
a servant of the church which is at Cenchrea; that you
receive her in the Lord in a manner worthy of the saints, and
that you help her in whatever matter she may have need of
you; for she herself has also been a helper of many, and of
myself as well.

Phoebe, the servant of the church in Cenchrea—the eastern
port of Corinth—had finished her journey. It had been a
long and dangerous trip, one that many men hesitated to
make.

Phoebe had traveled over land and over water. Her feet
had blistered from her endless walks over rocky, moun-
tainous roads. Her nerves had been tested when she crossed
from Macedonia to Italy in a creaky little ship. But under
all these circumstances she always remained conscious of
her task. She had to deliver Paul's letter to the Christians in
Rome undamaged.

*Taken from *Single & Human* by Ada Lum, page 40. Copyright © 1976 by Inter-
Varsity Christian Fellowship and used by permission of InterVarsity Press.

Finally the contours of the city rose up before her eyes. Rome, the eternal city, lay on its seven hills before her. The Appian Road on which she was walking led into the very heart of the city. For Phoebe, this trip was an exciting adventure in more ways than one.

Through this trip, first of all, her perspective had been extended. It was around A.D. 57, still the time when few people were privileged to travel and most of the travelers were men. It would take centuries before the world—first through the written word and later by means of modern mass media—would be broken open. People still lived in isolation and usually did not know many people outside their own cities.

This trip did not only allow Phoebe to visit another country and one of the most fascinating cities of all times; it also gave her the opportunity to meet other Christians. Apart from sharing the same faith, these Christians differed from her in many ways.

Phoebe was a single woman, but she was not lonely. Her life was anything but empty. Her fulfillment stemmed from her willingness to serve. By giving of herself to others, Phoebe kept the specter of loneliness at a distance. She knew that living for others draws people, particularly single people, out of their isolation. Being open to meet the needs of others helped make her life full and rich, an interesting and varied adventure.

Phoebe would experience that principle in Rome. The Christians there would not receive her as a stranger. Paul's scroll of parchment, her most precious baggage, contained a warm endorsement for the messenger. So she would be met with cordial interest and would be treated with honor.

"Help her in every way you can," Paul had written.[1] Phoebe, who was always thinking of other people, now would be helped herself. These words witnessed to Paul's loyal friendship and respect for Phoebe.

Paul, who had to postpone his visit to Rome many times,[2] dared to make his first contact with the Roman Christians through Phoebe. It would be three more years before he

1. Romans 16:1-2
2. Romans 1:13

would be able to visit Rome himself. Until that time, the Roman Church would see him through the eyes of Phoebe.

A prominent Christian leader, Paul put his reputation in the hands of a woman. It was risky for him to become so dependent on another person. With Phoebe, however, Paul dared to take the risk. He knew that she had a good reputation and would represent him. She had proved that she had a heart for God and His service. She was capable, dignified, and could be trusted to carry this great responsibility.

In Paul's letter to the Romans lay his most complete declaration of the Gospel. From the city of Rome the message of Christ would spread into the world. In that letter, Paul explained all the basic principles of the Gospel. He wanted his readers to know that every human being is a sinner.[3] He is born of sinful parents[4] and does sinful deeds, both of which deserve the death penalty. Without any exception, man without God is lost.[5] He is a creature that cannot exist before a holy God.[6] This is indeed the darkest fact of human history.

Paul's letter, however, did not only point to the greatest problem of humanity; it also contained God's great solution. Man did not need to suffer that terrible punishment. He was not condemned to die for his sin. He could escape his frightful destiny by appealing to the God-sent Mediator.

Jesus Christ—God's Son—underwent the death penalty even though He was innocent.[7] He gives complete pardon to people who accept His substitutionary work[8] and acknowledge that they are sinners. They must also believe and put their trust in Jesus Christ and publicly declare their decision for Christ.[9]

A person who believes and responds to Christ's message will not be condemned to spiritual death. Instead of being eternally separated from God, he will receive a new, eternal, and spiritual life. He becomes a child of God, and the Holy Spirit will give him a deep inner conviction of this truth.[10]

Continuing to build on the foundation of faith, Paul instructed the Romans about the assurance of salvation.[11] He talked about walking with God and living through the

---

3. Romans 3:23
4. Romans 5:12
5. Romans 6:23

6. Romans 3:10-18
7. Romans 5:8
8. Romans 8:1

9. Romans 10:9-10
10. Romans 8:16-17
11. Romans 8:31-39

power of the Holy Spirit. These and other great truths Paul defined in the letter that Phoebe, a willing servant of the Gospel, was taking to Rome.

The Bible doesn't tell how Phoebe herself came to a personal faith in Christ. The 49 words that describe her life are all too few. But her faith was certainly the content of her life and the motivation of her actions. She was a sister in the church where faith in Christ bound all the believers together into one large cross-cultural family. They met one another's needs like brothers and sisters.

With Phoebe, the word sister did not only point to a mutual, spiritual relationship; it also spoke of status. In a society in which the woman was placed far below the man, Phoebe took her place in the large family of the children of God in a completely equal spiritual relationship. From that position she began serving the church.

Serving for Phoebe was not giving herself to an inferior task. It was not a second-rate fulfillment of life. It became a grand privilege. In the port of Cenchrea, which like every major seaport showed sin in its crudest form, Phoebe's personality radiated light. Was it Phoebe's? No, the light of Jesus Christ[12] shone through her. Her light was a reflection of His transforming power.

We do not know how she helped others. Did she open up her home for the church like Lydia and Priscilla? Did she offer hospitality to people traveling eastward or westward through the seaport at the Aegean Sea? Or had her help consisted mainly of giving money and goods? These questions have no certain answers. They also are not very important, for we know that Phoebe's services were manifold, sacrificial, and effective.

Phoebe had no husband. She stood in life alone. Yet she was not waiting patiently for someone to relieve her loneliness. She used her solitude to serve others. *Who,* she may have thought, *can do this as unhindered as I? Who can give herself better to others than she who only has to take care of herself?*

That attitude also determined her relationship toward

Paul. There is no doubt that to Phoebe, Paul was the great apostle, God's servant. But he was also her "brother." He was a man who also stood alone in life, who needed and appreciated the help of an understanding woman.

Thus it worked out to be an ideal interaction. Whether Phoebe was placed in a special function—that of a deaconess, for instance—or whether she limited herself to unofficial service, we cannot know for sure. The first duty could be derived from the term "servant of the church," the second from the fact that she personally helped Paul and others. But for a woman like Phoebe, this made no difference. She was concerned about things that really mattered—her usefulness to God and other people. Such a servant had little desire for a title. She only wanted to be a human being with a positive influence. She commanded respect because of her faith and vision and because of her total giving of herself to others.

Every woman needs love and attention. Phoebe was no exception. She received what she needed by first giving her love and talents to others. To use Solomon's words, she was "enriched" because she first "gave freely."[13]

According to the laws of the kingdom of God, when Christians freely give they receive back abundantly. A person who does not hold back in serving—who joyously and voluntarily spreads love and friendship—will experience God's blessing. "God," Paul writes, "loves a cheerful giver."[14] On such a person He will heap good gifts. Such a person will always have more than enough, in every way; he will have overflowing means to do all kinds of good works.

The question whether humanity would have a copy of Paul's letter to the Romans if Phoebe had failed is mere speculation. God—the Eternal, the Sovereign, the Almighty One—was not dependent on a human being for the delivery of His message. But the fact remains that He used Phoebe to bring this precious Word of God to the Roman people and to the world.

Phoebe walked in front of a procession of women who through the ages have served Christ and His church. Paul

13. Proverbs 11:24-25
14. 2 Corinthians 9:6-8

mentioned her first in a long list of co-laborers, among which eight other women are named.[15]

Phoebe, the servant of the church at Cenchrea, showed every person—single or not—the effectual medicine against loneliness: serving.

Phoebe, a single woman who possessed the antidote to loneliness
(Romans 16:1-2)

Questions:
1. In your own words describe Paul's characterization of Phoebe. As you study questions 2-6, formulate some basic principles of the Gospel from the letter to the Romans, adding Bible references of your own choice to the answers.
2. Study Romans 3:10-18, 23; 6-23.
   a. Who have sinned?
   b. What is the penalty for sin?
3. How can a person receive pardon for his sin? (Romans 5:8; 8:1)
4. According to Romans 10:9-11, what conditions have to be met in order for a person to receive salvation?
5. Who convinces a Christian that he is a child of God? (Romans 8:16-17)
6. Ask yourself the following questions: In light of the above facts, am I a child of God? If so, what am I doing to share this message with others? If not, what can I do to become one? (Read John 1:12; 3:16; 14:6; and 1 John 5:11-12.)

---

15. Romans 16:1-16

*"The Lord Jesus was a living reality to me. In the
time I was still very young my mother told me how
dearly He loved children and how He wanted to live
in their hearts. I must have asked Him to come in,
though I don't know how and when."**
Corrie ten Boom

Lois and Eunice,
women who were convinced of the power
of God's Word

2 Timothy 1:5 For I am mindful of the sincere faith within you,
which first dwelt in your grandmother Lois, and your mother
Eunice, and I am sure that it is in you as well.

2 Timothy 3:14-17 You, however, continue in the things you
have learned and become convinced of, knowing from
whom you have learned them; and that from childhood you
have known the sacred writings which are able to give you
the wisdom that leads to salvation through faith which is in
Christ Jesus. All Scripture is inspired by God and profitable
for teaching, for reproof, for correction, for training in
righteousness; that the man of God may be adequate,
equipped for every good work.

Acts 16:1-3 And he came also to Derbe and to Lystra. And
behold, a certain disciple was there, named Timothy, the son
of a Jewish woman who was a believer, but his father was a
Greek, and he was well spoken of by the brethren who were
in Lystra and Iconium. Paul wanted this man to go with him;
and he took him and circumcised him because of the Jews

**Taken from *In Hem geborgen (Hidden in Him)* by Corrie ten Boom, page 15.
Published by Evangelische Lektuur Kruistocht, Almelo, The Netherlands. Used
by permission.*

who were in those parts for they all knew that his father was a Greek.

The names of Lois and Eunice cannot be separated. This is not because they were mother and daughter, but because of their sincere faith and view of the Holy Scriptures. Most important of all, though, they had mutual interest in Timothy, the son of Eunice and the grandson of Lois.

Their names occur only once in the Bible. But one must not, from that fact alone, jump to the conclusion that their lives were unimportant or that their influence was relatively small. The opposite is true. Their names are forever written down in history because of the indelible impression they made on the Apostle Paul, one of the greatest evangelists and the writer of much of the New Testament, including two letters to Timothy.

Around A.D. 67, Paul included these words in his last letter to Timothy from Rome: "I am calling up memories of your sincere and unqualified faith," he wrote, "the leaning of your entire personality on God in Christ in absolute trust and confidence in His power, wisdom and goodness, a faith that first lived permanently in the heart of your grandmother Lois and your mother Eunice and now, I am fully persuaded, dwells in you also."[1]

The persecution of Christians had begun during Emperor Nero's reign some years before and had culminated in a terrible fire that the emperor started himself but for which he blamed the Christians. That way he was able to give himself an excuse to persecute them.

Tradition states that Paul fell victim to that persecution. Imprisoned in Rome and waiting for his death, he wrote to his "son in the faith," Timothy.[2] He was looking forward with great desire to seeing his faithful and beloved co-laborer one last time.[3]

Paul knew that his earthly life was almost finished. His service was nearly completed. But through Timothy (and others) the work he had started would continue. In this

1. 2 Timothy 1:5
2. 2 Timothy 1:2
3. 2 Timothy 4:9

letter, the man who had accompanied him on so many trips—the co-laborer he had sent to different churches—would receive final instructions from his leader and teacher. These instructions would help Timothy to execute the task he and others were taking over from Paul.

The reason that Paul could write that he had fought the good fight and that he was living in the expectation of receiving the crown of righteousness[4] also had to do with Timothy.

Paul was convinced that the spiritual education and help he had given Timothy would not stop there, for Timothy had already proven that he took the lessons he had learned to heart. Once again Paul directed him toward the tasks which lay ahead. "For you must teach others those things you and many others have heard me speak about," Paul wrote. "Teach these great truths to trustworthy men who will, in turn, pass them on to others."[5]

As far as Paul was concerned, that teaching had started about 20 years earlier in Lystra. There he had briefly met Timothy while he was preaching during what was probably his first visit to that part of the world.[6]

From the beginning Paul had been struck by the boy's noble character and his God-fearing walk of life. Timothy, Paul found, had a good reputation with both the local Christians and those in nearby Iconium. With proper training, he could become a useful instrument in the service of God, for he had been taught in the Holy Scriptures since he was a small child.

However excellent Timothy's biblical education by his mother and grandmother might have been, it could not replace conversion. That remained indispensable. Therefore Timothy first had to be converted. Shortly after Timothy's conversion to Christ, Paul began to look after him, carefully training him in the service of God.

Timothy's initial instruction, however, had not started with Paul. Rather, it stemmed from the training begun years before under the direction of Lois and Eunice. Paul reaped what others had sown.

4. 2 Timothy 4:7-8
5. 2 Timothy 2:2
6. Acts 14:6-7

When the boy was born, his parents named him Timothy, which meant "he that fears God." But that name probably was chosen more by his Jewish mother than by his Greek father.

Why the God-fearing Eunice married a heathen man remains a secret. It is not known whether this happened with or without Lois' consent. Maybe both women were not Christians at that time. But whatever the case, Eunice's husband didn't personally encounter the God in whom she believed. Consequently Timothy remained uncircumcised.

Did the father die at an early age? Is that why the boy's education had to be undertaken by the mother? Did Eunice, being a widow, have to earn a living and therefore turn her son's education over to his grandmother?

Timothy thus was trained in the Holy Scriptures. That instruction was an invaluable privilege for which he never could thank God enough. He owed his religious education to his mother and grandmother. From his earliest childhood, he had been taught the Word of God.

Lois and Eunice didn't think, *Let's raise him "neutrally" and then later he can make his own decisions.* Nor did they reason, *He is still too young. Later, when he can understand things better, we will start training him in the Word.*

Lois and Eunice attached great value to the Bible themselves, and they took every opportunity to confront the boy early and thoroughly with it. Mother and grandmother did not only instill theoretical knowledge in Timothy. Day after day they showed him through their own lives how faith had to be applied in practice. This helped determine his character.

Of course they could go no further in their instruction than their knowledge reached. Being Jewish women living in a foreign land, they probably didn't know more than the content of the Old Testament. The message that the expected Messiah had come in the person of Jesus of Nazareth and that He was offering forgiveness of sin was not entirely clear to them. The news that God had become available to everyone who believed in Christ were facts that became known through the messages of Paul.

However deeply the faith of the mother and grandmother had penetrated the life of the boy, it didn't save him. He himself had to come to a personal choice for Jesus Christ. Like Paul, he had to believe that Jesus Christ came into the world to save sinners.[7] He also had to accept that he was a sinner.

The future messenger of the Gospel first had to believe the Gospel himself. He had to believe that Jesus Christ died, was buried, and raised from the dead according to the Scriptures.[8] He had to turn his life over to Christ on a personal level.

When Paul arrived in Lystra years before, God proved the truth of the prophecy of Isaiah. His Word would not return empty; it would accomplish a work He purposed to do.[9] Timothy, the son of Eunice and the grandson of Lois, became the "son in the Lord" of Paul. The apostle became his father in Christ Jesus through the Gospel.[10]

Because the mother and the grandmother through the Holy Spirit's power had sown that Word generously in the receptive heart of a young child, it resulted in new birth after Paul's preaching.[11]

Did Lois and Eunice possibly plead with God concerning the words of their former, illustrious King Solomon who had written, "Train up a child in the way he should go, and when he is old he will not depart from it"?[12]

Timothy first became a Christian and then an active messenger of Jesus Christ, an ambassador for God.[13] He became a man who would tell people the good news of the Gospel.[14] His life gained eternal value. He was a wise man who "shall shine like the brightness of the firmament," because he "turned many to righteousness."[15]

What mother, what grandmother could expect richer fruit of her teaching? How intensely grateful this mother and grandmother must have been when Timothy began his task of preaching the Gospel. By instructing Timothy in the laws of the Hebrews, Lois and Eunice did not only lay a foundation for Timothy's conversion; they also prepared

7. 1 Timothy 1:15; Acts 16:31

8. 1 Corinthians 15:1-4

9. Isaiah 55:11

10. 1 Corinthians 4:15, 17

11. 1 Peter 1:23

12. Proverbs 22:6

13. 2 Corinthians 5:20

14. 2 Timothy 4:5

15. Daniel 12:3

him for his life's work.

When he, still only a lad, left Lystra with Paul to replace Paul's former co-laborer Barnabas, a heavy task was waiting for him. He would make long trips that might break his basically weak constitution. He would become entangled in difficulties against which his sensitive and timid nature would hardly be equal.

Timothy would need the Word of God, which Lois and Eunice had given him, every day of his life. He would have to stick to it, live by it, and use it as a preparation for eternity. He could not do without it in everyday living. It was his comfort, his strength, his compass.

In order to be a servant of God, up to his task and equipped to do all good work, Timothy would take the Word for his guidance. He would be instructed and corrected by it. It would continue to educate him toward a godly character. The Word Timothy had learned to love and obey in the home would also inspire him, and prove to be a necessary instrument in training others in biblical truth.

The link of faith from Lois to Eunice to Timothy didn't stop there. Through Timothy, many other people would come to embrace the same faith and would be stimulated and instructed to preach the Gospel. He remained a co-laborer with Paul till Paul's death, and the fact that Paul asked Timothy to come to Rome to comfort him in his last earthly hours shows the affection which bound them.[16]

Eunice and Lois naturally did not know the great plans God had for Timothy. Monica, likewise, did not know which role her son, Augustine, would play in church history. The mother of Billy Graham could not suspect how many people would become Christians through her son's ministry. God has wonderful surprises for people, mothers and grandmothers, who are trusting God to bless their loved ones.

How easily the lives of Lois and Eunice—two inconspicuous women who lived in Asia Minor (present-day Turkey)—could have remained anonymous.

Since they lived the Bible has been translated into hundreds of languages and distributed in millions of copies. Until this day, Bible readers the world over continue to meet

16. 2 Timothy 4:9

Lois and Eunice, two women who were convinced of the power of God's Word and the influence of it on a human life.

Lois and Eunice, women who were convinced of the power of God's Word
(2 Timothy 1:5; 3:14-17; Acts 16:1-3)

Questions:
1. In what ways was Timothy strongly influenced by his mother and grandmother? Try to determine their influence.
2. When did Timothy first learn the Holy Scriptures? How did he use this knowledge?
3. According to 2 Timothy 3:16-17, how does Scripture prepare a person for God's service?
4. As Timothy grew older, what things did he do in the service of God? (You may want to go through passages in the New Testament and develop a character study of Timothy.)
5. What did you learn from Lois and Eunice concerning instruction of the Word of God?
6. Write down the principle you believe to be most important in this story and then list ways in which you can apply it in your life or in the lives of others around you.

**If you enjoyed *Her Name Is Woman,
Book 2,* then *The Life and Ministry of Jesus
Christ, Design for Discipleship,* and
Her Name Is Woman, Book 1 are for you.**

The Life and Ministry of Jesus Christ is a three-book Bible study series produced by an experienced Navigator team after extensive field-testing. It is a chronological study of all four Gospels, examining everything that Jesus said and did. The study requires a person to dig deeply into the Word in serious individual preparation, and includes background material about the culture, geography, and history of Jesus' times. It stresses personal application of the timeless truths learned, and aids the person in his Christian growth and walk.

Design for Discipleship is for the person who wants to become a Christ-centered disciple—who does not accept everything he hears, but wants to know what God says in His Word. Scripture often discusses the same subject in more than one passage. The *Design for Discipleship* series draws these major teachings on a subject together and then asks penetrating questions to aid in understanding. "Questions for Meditation" are provided for those who desire to go still deeper in their understanding of God's Word.

Her Name Is Woman, Book 1, Gien Karssen's first book, explores the fascinating stories of 24 women of the Bible and emphasizes practical ways in which readers can apply the biblical principles found in the chapters.